DATHA WILSON WHITFIELD

The Messy Marvelous Middle

FINDING JESUS IN UNEXPECTED PLACES

BROOKSTONE
PUBLISHING GROUP

Birmingham, Alabama

The Messy Marvelous Middle

Brookstone Publishing Group
An imprint of Iron Stream Media
100 Missionary Ridge
Birmingham, AL 35242
IronStreamMedia.com

Library of Congress Control Number has been requested.

Scripture quotations, unless otherwise indicated, are taken from The Holy Bible, New International Version®, NIV®. Copyright © 1973, 1978, 1984, 2011 by Biblica, Inc. Used with permission of Zondervan. All rights reserved worldwide. www.zondervan.com

Scripture quotations marked MSG are taken from The Message, copyright © 1993, 2002, 2018 by Eugene H. Peterson. Used by permission of NavPress. All rights reserved. Represented by Tyndale House Publishers.

Cover design by www.BookCoverDesign.us

ISBN: 978-1-960814-22-7 (paperback)
ISBN: 978-1-960814-23-4 (eBook)

1 2 3 4 5—30 29 28 27 26

"As you read *The Messy Marvelous Middle*, you feel like you're sitting in a comfortable, honest conversation with the girl next door. Through personal stories, scripture, biblical truth, and thoughtful reflection questions, Datha invites readers into the often-messy middle of life with hope and freedom promised from God. The book gently reframes the common belief that God will never give us more than we can handle, showing instead that He may give us more than we can handle in order to draw us into deeper dependence on Him. He will never give us more than He can handle through us. By sharing how she hears from God and prays from an ongoing, authentic relationship with Him, the author creates a book that feels real, encouraging, and deeply relatable; one that meets you right where you are in your own messy middle and reminds you that God is present and at work."

—Anna Nash, author of *Refreshing Hospitality*, *Christmas Matters*, and *Easter Matters*

"Have you ever found yourself in an ordinary season when you pray, 'God, things are a little messy, and I need to see you.' Datha reminds us that God does holy work in ordinary seasons. Datha's writing has a bit of southern sass mixed with sweet wisdom. Her writing takes you right along with her as she shares her memories. Datha will leave you wanting more."

—Janet Hart Leonard, author of *When the Hart Speaks: Whimsy and Wisdom from the Little House on the Alley*

"*The Messy Marvelous Middle* is just what its title states. It's marvelous! The book is filled with emotional stories that will resonate with women, and Datha's deep knowledge will give them hope within the messiness of life."

—Cheryl Wray, Author & Coordinator of the Southern Christian Writers Conference

"The messy, marvelous middle will appear on your tombstone as a dash. In this book, Datha invites you to extend that line—one day, even one breath, at a time. Her transparency makes her relatable; her hard-won milestones give her authority. As her stories draw you in, her questions release you to see your messes as scenes in a providential story—full of design and meaning. You will read until you laugh, read until you cry, read until you pray—and find yourself praying long after the final page. Dear reader, you are about to see your dash in a time-altering way."

—Melvin Airhart (Coach Mel), Founder & Director, Principio Coaching

To the love of my life . . . my husband.
To my beautiful children . . .
I love you each endlessly and equally.

CONTENTS

Contents

PREFACE

I didn't write this book from a mountaintop. I wrote it from the middle.

The middle of unanswered prayers.

The middle of dreams that took longer than expected.

The middle of laughing one minute and crying the next.

The middle of putting my trust in God while also screaming into a pillow.

For a long time, I thought I had messed up, missed God, or fallen behind everyone else. But slowly, and sometimes painfully, I learned something life-changing:

God does holy work in ordinary seasons.

He heals in hidden places.

He builds strength in silence.

He fulfills promises even when nothing looks finished.

This book was born from journal pages, conversations, memories, family, road trips, counseling sessions, early mornings with Jesus, hotel lobbies, Mexican spas (yes, that happened), and every messy, marvelous moment in between.

If you are in a season that feels unfinished, uncomfortable, uncertain, or unseen—this is for you. I hope these pages remind you that you are not alone, you are not forgotten, and your story is nowhere near done.

And to every woman who ever prayed, "God, I'm trying . . . but I need You to meet me here," He will. He always does.

INTRODUCTION

Everybody loves beginnings.

Fresh starts. New chapters. Big dreams.

We also love endings . . . victories, breakthroughs, happily ever afters.

But what about the middle.

The middle is where faith is stretched.

Where identity shifts.

Where the miracle is still in motion but the finish line is nowhere in sight.

Maybe you're there right now, between "God, I thought by now . . ." and "Lord, I'm still believing."

This book isn't about having a perfect life. It's about finding a perfect God in the imperfect places. Together, we'll laugh, cry, heal, pray, rethink, breathe, hope, and chase down God's promises like they belong to us—because they do.

Here's what you'll find in these pages:

- stories from real life—the kind women usually only tell each other in the kitchen or the car ride home;
- biblical truth that speaks to the heart, not the highlight reel;
- reflection questions to help you process what God is doing right where you are; and
- permission to stop pretending and start healing.

By the end, you'll discover something powerful: The middle is not the part you survive. It's the part where God writes your testimony.

Your life may feel messy, but God is still marvelous—and He's not finished with you yet.

CHAPTER 1

THE DAY I JUMPED

July 17, 2015. My last day at Princeton Hospital in Birmingham, Alabama.

I turned to my coworker, Emily, and asked her to walk with me to the front entrance. I had already turned in my notice weeks before, and I wanted to mark this moment with a photo. Dressed in my bright coral scrubs, I stood in front of the hospital sign, determined to capture the day. The traffic was constant, the intersection buzzing with cars from the McDonald's across the street, and I'm sure I looked a little ridiculous to the passersby. But I didn't care. This day was one of the most significant of my life.

From the moment I held my first baby, my heart longed to be a stay-at-home mom. But, like so many mothers, that dream felt out of reach.

Jason and I married young—he had just graduated high school, and I had only one year of college under my belt. Seven months later, we welcomed an eight-pound, eight-ounce baby boy—Jordan Bo. (More on his arrival in a later chapter.) I will never forget the way my world shifted the moment I held him. His tiny fingers, his chunky leg rolls, his perfect little chin—I wanted to spend every moment just staring at him.

Those first few months, I barely let anyone else hold him. I was young and inexperienced, determined to learn how to be the best mother I could be. My only babysitting experience as a teenager had ended in disaster— a toddler covered in lipstick, a pitcher of Kool-Aid spilled across the floor, and a baby sent to bed with her shoes still on because I couldn't figure out how to take them off. (Dang high-top walkers with bells) But now, this was my baby, and I was going to figure it out.

When Jordan Bo turned one, I decided to pick up a few days of work. I enrolled him in daycare, dropped him off, then went back home to get ready. But something in me couldn't let go, so I stopped back by the daycare to check on him. What I saw shattered me—my little boy, sitting in the corner, red-faced and crying. I didn't even hesitate. I scooped him up and started walking towards the door.

"He won't be back," I declared. The daycare employees tried to assure me that he just had to adjust to his new routine, but I could not stand the thought of him crying all day while he adjusted to his surroundings. So back home we went.

I stayed home with him until he was almost three, and we pinched pennies, and my husband worked two jobs. Then I started nursing school. Two years later, I graduated—now a mom to a five-year-old and a five-month-old. I took a full-time job, and for years, Jason and I carefully balanced opposite shifts so one of us could always be with the kids. Family and close friends helped, but my heart was always at home. No matter how much I loved aspects of nursing, I lived for the moment I could clock out and rush back to my babies—even when those babies had become teenagers.

And then, our surprise blessing arrived—a baby girl. With her, the pull to be home was stronger than ever.

In 2014, Jason lost one of his jobs, and in a single day, half of our income was gone. Bills piled up. The weight of stress sat heavily on our shoulders as we both searched for solutions. I accepted an offer at an after-hours clinic to make up for the lost income, but the thought of spending weekends away from my family crushed me.

One evening in April 2014, just days before I was set to start, I sat in our den, scrolling aimlessly through Facebook. That's when I saw it. A simple post that offered information about making extra money—something you could do from your phone at home.

A small whisper stirred inside me, nudging me to reach out to the person who had posted it. That single moment set off a chain of events I never could have imagined.

What I thought was just a desperate attempt to make extra income became something so much bigger. It led me to something I genuinely loved, in an industry that felt exciting and rewarding.

Fourteen months later, I stood in front of that hospital sign, feeling the rush of adrenaline as Emily snapped a few quick pictures on my iPhone. Then—without thinking—I jumped.

Looking back, I see the symbolism.

I had taken a leap into the unknown, chasing a dream I thought was impossible. And I landed exactly where my heart had always longed to be—at home.

Now, over ten years later, I still look at that photo and remember the day I jumped. It was the beginning of something I never saw coming—an unfolding of purpose in the most unexpected place. It hasn't always been easy, but it's been the most incredible, wild, fun, and challenging journey—a journey of unexpected opportunities, of dreams being reborn, of God's faithfulness stamped on every step. It's the day I chose to keep dreaming.

And I am living proof of this truth:

"God can do anything, you know—far more than you could ever imagine or guess or request in your wildest dreams."

---

1. Is there a dream or longing in your heart that feels impossible? How can you trust God to make a way, even when the path seems unclear?

2. Think of a time when you had to take a leap of faith. How did you see God's faithfulness in that season, and how can that encourage you in your current circumstances?

CHAPTER 2

LOVE STORY

On August 12, 1988, my first child arrived in the world—twenty-eight weeks and six days after a "shotgun wedding." It's comical to think of my wedding that way.

Shotgun Wedding: A term for a wedding that happens quickly, often because the bride is unexpectedly pregnant. The phrase comes from the idea that the bride's family (historically, the father) might pressure the groom into marriage to ensure the child is born within wedlock.

Now, don't get me wrong—I was unexpectedly pregnant, and my wedding happened quickly. But the timeline is a bit foggy to me. Between the moment I found out I was pregnant and the moment I walked down the aisle, just a few months had passed, but no one was pressured. The moment I shared the news with my eighteen-year-old boyfriend, he immediately, without hesitation, said, "Let's get married!"

We had dated for several years, and I had a little heart-shaped promise ring on my finger that he had given me at Captain D's Restaurant over a basket of fish and chips. Yes, I'm giggling as

I type this. We were so in love. Although he lived in Hueytown, Alabama, with his parents, and I lived in Clinton, Mississippi, with mine, our number one goal was to be together.

Our love story began when we were children. We were both invited to be in the same wedding—I was the junior bridesmaid, and Jason was the junior groomsman. We were eleven and twelve years old, and apparently, it was love at first sight. He was beanpole thin, wearing a bow tie almost as big as his head, with the most mischievous grin. I had crooked teeth, big glasses, and wore a blue dotted swiss hoop skirt with a matching umbrella. Imagine a classic '80s antebellum wedding explosion.

We walked down the aisle together that day, August 2, 1980, and then spent the rest of the evening chasing each other around the parking lot. Over the next few years, we saw each other once, exchanged lots of letters, and then, as teenagers, reconnected in December 1985. I was a senior in high school living in Clinton, Mississippi.

That December day is one I'll never forget. Jason arrived with his sister and her husband (the same couple whose wedding we had been in years earlier). I watched from the house next door, where my cousins lived, as he got out of the car and walked inside. I remember the moment like it was yesterday. Peeking out the bedroom window, I saw him for the first time in years. He was wearing a long-sleeved button-up shirt, Levi's that were tight-rolled, and high-top sneakers. And he was so good-looking. My heart definitely skipped a beat.

I gathered my courage and walked next door. I remember thinking, Do I hug him? Shake his hand? Talk about awkward. I'm pretty sure we hugged, but it's all a blur. What I do remember is staying up until the early hours of the morning talking—and then doing it again the next night. We went to the movies, went to church, and talked a lot. We also kissed (sorry, kids—don't read this part). But it was butterflies galore, fireworks, and a heck yeah!

After a few days, he went back home, but our worlds had shifted. Our only goal was to see each other and talk as much as possible. This was before cell phones and social media, and long-distance calls were expensive, so we started writing letters. Recently, I counted the letters I've kept in a beautiful wooden box—450 letters written over two years.

We tried to see each other as often as possible. Thankfully, my dad was pastoring in Mississippi, so we were only a four-hour drive apart. We went to prom together, youth trips, and graduations. Sometimes, we would meet halfway in Meridian at McDonald's just to spend a few hours together. We were young and dumb, so those two years also included arguments, but we were deeply in love.

Our love created a beautiful, perfect baby. There's no better way to say it. But it also created challenges. I was scared. My boyfriend wanted to marry me. He had a job that paid $5 an hour. I didn't want to tell my parents. I had no idea what to do.

I grabbed a phone book, looked up "pregnancy center," and drove there to confirm the pregnancy. Sitting in the waiting room, I silently wept. The nurse confirmed the pregnancy and handed me a pamphlet with pictures of babies at different stages of development. I walked to my car alone, sat in the parking lot, and cried.

I have absolutely no memory of what happened over the next few weeks and months. It's a complete blur. I just remember feeling scared, ashamed, and confused. I know I called Jason and told him the news. I know I had a hard conversation with my parents. I know we hugged and cried. They told me how much they loved me and comforted me—no reprimands, no criticism, no looks of disappointment. Just love.

Dad asked what we wanted to do, and I blurted out, "Get married."

My mother and Aunt Lou planned every detail of the wedding in lovely shades of peach and blue. My Uncle Jerry and Aunt Trisha gave me money for a wedding dress—1980s perfection with puffy sleeves, a high neck, and a drop waist. Jason wore a white tux with tails, and the highlight of the wedding was my sister and cousin, Rynn and Landy, singing "Just You and I."

We left our wedding for a short honeymoon in Gatlinburg, and I was so tired. I had no idea I was "first-trimester tired." I hadn't even been to a doctor yet.

Looking back, I know I felt like I was in the middle of my biggest mistake. But in reality, it was my greatest blessing—the arrival of Jordan Bo Whitfield. My perfect baby boy, who grew into an incredible man of God. He brought so much joy and laughter, so much growth and challenge. My firstborn. An anointed man of God.

Sometimes what feels like your biggest mistake is actually the place where God begins to rewrite your story. It's in those unexpected places that we start reclaiming purpose—and find the courage to keep dreaming.

"And we know that in all things God works for the good of those who love Him, who have been called according to His purpose" (Romans 8:28).

---

1. Have you ever experienced a situation that felt like a mistake but later turned out to be a blessing? How did you see God's hand at work in it?

2. Romans 8:28 reminds us that God works all things for good. How can you trust Him more fully with the uncertainties or challenges in your life today?

CHAPTER 3

THE POOL

After picking up my baby boy from daycare and vowing never to leave him again, we entered a glorious era I like to call "poverty leisure." That's when you're living on next to nothing but still determined to have a good time. Our new headquarters? A cozy (translation: tiny) two-bedroom, one-bath rental house. My young husband worked tirelessly to keep us afloat while I stayed home with little Jordan Bo, filling our days with whatever entertainment I could scrape together.

With a very creative budget for fun, I settled on three main activities:

1. MTV—because music videos and questionable fashion choices were free.
2. Step aerobics—a few budget-friendly classes to convince myself I was staying active.
3. The community pool—aka my personal tanning salon and entertainment for Jordan Bo.

The Pleasant Grove Community Pool was a goldmine. For just a little change, we could spend the day swimming (Jordan) and sunbathing (me). Several times a week, I'd pack my toddler some snacks , scrounge up some coins from the couch cushions, and head to the pool.

That's where I often met up with Tammy—Jason's cousin and my fellow "poverty leisure" enthusiast. Our kids played while we lay out and baked under the Alabama sun, swapping stories and dreaming about our futures. Tammy was fun, chatty, and slightly ahead of me in life because—get this—she and her husband were getting a new mattress. A brand-new mattress.

Out of the kindness of her heart (and possibly because they didn't want to pay dump fees), Tammy offered us their old one. "You can have it, but just know, you'll be sleeping around the springs," she warned, as if this were some kind of exclusive, rustic experience. But hey, free is free, and I was honestly impressed they were moving up in the world. Maybe we were next in line for upward mobility.

Another beloved "poverty leisure" activity was game nights with other young couples. Since our house was way too small, we'd gather at David and Kim's or Bobby and Linda's, where we played games for hours while our kids ran wild, turning each host's home into a disaster zone.

Looking back, I smile at that season. Jason was working two jobs, which made me sad because I felt like I should contribute somehow. And then one fateful day at the Pleasant Grove Community Pool, Tammy and I had a life-altering conversation.

Tammy: I think I'm gonna go back to school or take some classes.

Me: Oh yeah? What ya thinking?

Tammy: Either cosmetology or nursing.

Me: Cool. You decide, get the info, and I'll go with you.

And just like that, without a single ounce of planning or deep reflection, I became a nurse.

A few months later, we walked into Bessemer Tech for our first day of nursing school. I had never—not once—considered nursing as a career path. I had tried college briefly after high school, but nothing stuck. Then came my shotgun wedding, and higher education was put on pause indefinitely. But here I was, following Tammy's decision like it was my own.

That impulsive decision turned into a twenty-year nursing career—from nursing homes to home care to doctors' offices. I worked some great jobs, met amazing coworkers (even worked with Tammy for a while), and, most importantly, cared for countless patients. I loved helping people—explaining a new diagnosis, easing someone's anxiety, or just being a kind presence. Oh, the stories I could tell . . . but, you know, HIPAA.

And yet . . . something never quite fit.

For almost my entire nursing career, Jason was pastoring a church (we'll get into that later), and oddly enough, being a pastor's wife? That fit. At twenty-nine, I accidentally stepped into a role I initially resisted but ended up absolutely loving—building community, planning events, forming deep friendships.

It was a season of raising kids, working hard, and juggling all the things. But even in the midst of it, I always felt that something was missing.

Do you ever want to go back and shake your twenty-year-old or thirty-year-old self? Like, girl, what are you doing?? Yeah. Same.

---

1. Have you ever made a major life decision without truly seeking God's guidance? Looking back, how might things have been different if you had invited Him into the process?

2. In seasons where you felt something "didn't fit," do you think God was trying to redirect you? What might He have been preparing you for?

CHAPTER 4

NKOTB

It was the early '90s, and New Kids on the Block were ruling the world—every teeny bopper on the planet was swooning over the fresh-faced, dance-move-slaying Boston boys. Everyone had a favorite—Jordan, Joey, Donnie, Danny, or Jonathan—and my sister Rynn was an ultrafan. And me? Well, let's just say I may have mildly appreciated their musical contributions.

One day, Rynn, still living at home in Louisiana, called me and asked me to drive over and take her and her best friend, Nadrid, to Shreveport to "stake out" (aka "track down like amateur private investigators") NKOTB. We had exactly one previous attempt at groupie life under our belts from when the New Kids came to Birmingham, Alabama—so obviously, we were experts now.

The only problem? I was in my "poverty leisure" era. Gas money was scarce, but my sister's dream was on the line, so I scraped together some change, hit the road, and arrived ready to embark on our totally foolproof mission. The plan? Find NKOTB, get Rynn's cassette tape of her singing directly into their hands, and watch as they are so utterly blown away by her talent that they immediately invite her to join the tour. Simple.

Now, let's talk about my outfit choice. I had on a purple fitted dress that hit just above the knee, accessorized with a giant chain belt, and my hair was teased to heights only achievable in Texas. Why? I don't know. I was just the driver, but apparently, I thought I needed to dress like I had front-row seats. Spoiler: We had no tickets—the concert had been sold out for months, and even if they had been available, I was way too broke for that level of commitment.

We rolled into downtown Shreveport and began our high-level detective work: driving around to all the fancy hotels, scanning for tour buses, paparazzi, or throngs of screaming fans. Just when we were about to lose hope, we hit the jackpot—one hotel had a massive crowd gathered outside. Bingo. We parked and joined the hysteria.

After a while, several mysterious white cargo vans with heavily tinted windows rolled out from behind the hotel, scattering in different directions. My elite investigative instincts kicked in: diversion tactic. The question was—do we stay put and hope for a tour bus sighting, or do we follow the vans? But which one?!

Then, in a stroke of luck, as one of the vans passed right in front of us, the sunlight hit its tinted windows just perfectly, revealing a shadowy figure inside. My sister shrieked "RATTAIL!!!" and that was all the confirmation we needed.

Rattail: A hairstyle that should have never existed but, for some reason, thrived in the '90s. A thin, regrettable strip of hair trailing down the back of one's head, often sported by boy band members and rebellious middle schoolers.

With the grace and strategy of an FBI pursuit team, we peeled out of the parking lot, joining several other deranged fans in a high-stakes chase through downtown traffic. The van was headed toward the stadium. Then, at a red light, my sister decided to take matters into her own hands.

She bolted from our car, ran straight to the van in the middle of a busy intersection, and started pounding on the side door!

Everything went into slow motion.

The door slid open . . . and there was Danny.

Was he our first choice? No. But was he a New Kid? YES. So we were ecstatic.

Through our shrieking, Rynn ran back to the car, breathless. "THE DOOR OPENED! IT WAS DANNY! He told me to get back in my car before I got run over, but I shoved my tape into his hands before the door closed!!"

Mission accomplished.

Or so we thought.

We followed the van until it disappeared behind the stadium gates, then pulled over, giddy but unsure what to do next. And then—out of nowhere—a security guard appeared.

He waved us in.

What in the world?!

I cautiously rolled down my window as we inched forward. The guard leaned in and said, "Danny wants to meet the girl who gave him the tape."

SCREAMING.

We parked and were led to the stadium's loading zone, where Danny himself was waiting. He motioned for Rynn to come over, while Nadrid and I stood back, eyes locked on the situation like a couple of nervous stage moms. After a few minutes, Danny slipped away through a nearby door, and Rynn came running back, grinning like she just won the lottery.

"He listened to my tape! He said I have an amazing voice!"

We lost our minds.

But then—plot twist—she admitted she told him we didn't even have tickets. And bless his heart, Danny disappeared again . . . only to reappear minutes later, handing us concert tickets AND backstage passes.

That night, we stood (because no one sat at a New Kids concert) in the third row of the Magic Summer Tour, singing along to "Valentine Girl," "You Got It (The Right Stuff)," "Please Don't Go Girl," "Hangin' Tough," "I'll Be Loving You (Forever)," and "Step by Step."

After the concert, we were escorted backstage, where we got to meet every single member of NKOTB and take pictures with them. I posed with Jordan, my actual favorite, and in the heat of the moment, my starstruck brain malfunctioned and blurted out—

"I NAMED MY BABY AFTER YOU!"

. . . which was (1) a complete lie and (2) probably terrifying for him to hear from a stranger in the middle of a meet-and-greet.

We drove home that night on cloud nine, thrilled that our mission had wildly exceeded our expectations. Rynn never heard from Danny, although he did have her phone number, and she invested in an answering machine to make sure she never missed a call! She never got invited to join the tour, and never became the next big pop star.

But she did get an epic story. And really, that was the next best thing.

---

1. Have you ever met someone you admired? How did you handle the moment—calm and collected or completely tongue-tied?

2. Have you ever stepped into an unexpected adventure that turned out even better than you imagined?

CHAPTER 5

RINGS & REDEMPTION, PART 1

Jason and I celebrated thirty-seven years of marriage last month. We are complete opposites in almost every way—like most couples, I imagine. Opposites attract, right? But where it matters most, we are exactly the same. We love Jesus. Our children are the most important part of our lives. We cherish quiet mornings with coffee, early bedtimes, and long drives in search of hidden-gem restaurants with the best food. Sundays are sacred—worshiping together at church and heading to our favorite restaurant afterward. And we love the water—not to swim in, but to sit beside, watch, and just be. Lakes, rivers, beaches . . . they bring us peace.

Through the years, our marriage has been steadfast, built on commitment, but that doesn't mean it's been easy. We've had our fair share of ups and downs, trials and struggles. I mean, if you've been married as long as we have and haven't packed up your things at least once, are you even married?

In our early years, I packed up my little gray Ford Taurus at least five times, determined to move back home to Louisiana. Thankfully, my parents moved closer to us, shortening my dramatic escape route. Not that it mattered—I never even made it to the interstate before turning around to make up. We argued a lot. Over what? I don't even remember, but it probably had something to do with our "poverty leisure" era—when I was focused on the leisure part instead of the poverty part. We were so young, with a new baby, just trying to figure it all out.

By year twelve, we had entered our WWF era—Worship, Work, and Family. Our entire lives revolved around those three things, and we wrestled constantly with how to balance them. Our little church was growing, and Jason, along with several other men, spent every evening after work at the new building site. The metal frame was up, but the rest was up to them—framing, drywall, painting, hanging doors. I often packed up dinner and brought the kids so we could eat together at the church. It was an exciting time, full of momentum and vision. We dreamed of a Christian school and a gym. But with all the excitement came strain—long hours away from home led to arguments.

One night, after another late shift hanging drywall, Jason came home and told me his wedding ring had slipped off somewhere in the building. It was lost—forever sealed inside those church walls. My immediate response? "Well, that makes sense. You're practically married to that building." It was more than irony to me.

Years later, while on vacation, my wedding rings were stolen. I've never been one for expensive jewelry, just a few sentimental pieces. My engagement ring was a simple quarter-carat solitaire on a gold band, purchased in 1988 from Loyle Seymore Jewelry in Bessemer, Alabama—the same store Jason's dad had once shopped for his wife. It was small, simple, and perfect. And now, it was gone too.

Now, we were both ringless.

For our twentieth anniversary, we made reservations at the beautiful Whitestone Country Inn in Kingston, Tennessee. Before heading out of town, we picked up two new gold bands we had ordered weeks earlier—thick, solid, and perfect. I had my heart set on a romantic ring exchange, and Jason, ever the good sport, went along with it. That night, standing on the balcony of our room overlooking a quiet lake, we slipped the rings onto each other's fingers, whispering words of love and commitment. It was a beautiful, sacred moment.

And standing there on that little balcony, we had no idea what was coming next.

Soon, those rings would be gone too.

---

1. When you look back over the different "eras" of your own marriage or relationships, which moments—both the peaceful and the messy—shaped you the most and why?

2. How have the changes, losses, or unexpected turns in your relationship invited you to grow, either in love, commitment, or the way you show up for each other?

CHAPTER 6

LOOK UP

My childhood was as unique as my name—Datha Suzanne. Born on July 24, 1968, in Jackson, Mississippi, my name's origin story began long before I took my first breath. My mother had another name in mind, but she settled on Datha. The story goes that my precious Maw-Maw, whom I adored, disliked the name my mother had chosen for me so much that she asked to pick a more "normal" middle name for me. She chose Suzanne. If you have ever been with me at a coffee shop or restaurant and I'm asked for a name, it's always Ann, an ode to Suzanne and the name my maw-maw gave me.

Now, Datha? People ask me all the time how to pronounce it, how to spell it, and where it came from. The answer is simple.

One humid Southern evening, my parents sat at Camp Meeting (a marathon of fiery preaching lasting at least a week). They were listening to one of those fiery preachers bring the Word, and at some point in his sermon, he casually mentioned his daughter's name—Datha. My mother leaned in, something about the name catching her attention. And just like that, the name she had originally chosen for me was erased.

What was it, you ask?

Jemima.

I kid you not. My mother, an avid reader of Western novels, had been inspired by Daniel Boone's daughter. But when she heard Datha, something inside her shifted. (Thank you, Jesus.) And just like that, I dodged a lifetime of syrup jokes.

But my unusual childhood wasn't just about my name.

My parents' love story began in Tupelo, Mississippi, where my dad was attending Bible school. One weekend, he traveled home with his friend Glenn Maughon, never suspecting that his future was waiting for him there—Glenn's eighteen-year-old sister, Charlotte. Sparks flew, and six months later, they were married. Their life together wasn't ordinary—it was a life of ministry, of planting churches, of traveling from city to city to spread the gospel.

By the time I graduated high school, I had attended seventeen different schools. At one point, I wasn't even homeschooled—I was car-schooled, learning my lessons between church services in whatever state we happened to be passing through. While other kids were planning family vacations, my childhood was marked by the ever-changing scenery of new towns, different congregations, and the constant rhythm of revivals. Some lasted days, others stretched into months. We stayed wherever we could—parsonages, apartments, the homes of pastors, with family, sometimes even in hotels.

But I never saw my life as unusual. It was all I knew. I always felt safe, always felt loved. My parents made sure of that.

Despite the unpredictability, my mom had a way of making our lives feel rich. She was the best cook—simple, Southern meals with biscuits and cornbread. She was endlessly creative, writing songs and playing the piano. My dad, a history buff, filled our travels with stories of the past, dragging us to presidential homes and historical sites. And my mother's deep love of music meant we were always singing. If you lived in our house, you had to know how to harmonize. And if you didn't? Well, you'd learn. Quickly.

Books were my escape, my adventure, my steady companions when everything else around me was constantly changing.

Being the new girl wasn't just a phase—it was a way of life. With every move came the same routine: stepping into an unfamiliar classroom, scanning the sea of faces, hoping for a kind glance, an open seat, a simple invitation. But I wasn't just the new girl—I was the new girl with the odd name who looked different from everyone else.

My parents were part of a religious organization that believed women shouldn't wear pants, makeup, or jewelry or cut their hair. So there I was, in a long skirt or dress, bare-faced, hair uncut since birth, sticking out like a prairie girl in a 90210 world. Middle school only made it worse—crooked teeth, big glasses, and the desperate desire to just blend in.

I'll never forget one particular day in seventh grade. As I walked to the bus, head down, shoulders slumped, my dad pulled me aside later that evening.

"Datha," he said, his voice gentle but firm, "I saw you walking with your head down today, and I didn't like that. I want you to walk with your head up."

His words hit me. What I heard wasn't just a command—it was a reminder.

"You may feel awkward. You may feel invisible. But I see you. You are beautiful. You are worthy. Lift your head."

That moment, that lesson, has stayed with me long after those awkward school days. Because isn't that what we're all searching for? A friend. A place to belong. A simple sign that we are seen.

At every new school, every new church, every new neighborhood—I always had a friend. God always provided someone. Some names I still remember: Dawn, Ann, Lora, Lesa, Janet, Sheila,

Tami. Others are just warm memories, familiar faces that made me feel included for a season.

And now, looking back, I realize something important: We all have the chance to be that person for someone else.

Maybe today, you are searching for belonging. Or maybe, you are the one who can offer it. Either way, I have two words for you—

LOOK UP.

Look up and see that God will bring the people you need.

Look up and notice the one who needs you.

Because friendship is often born in the simplest of moments—when one person looks at another and says,

"What? You too? I thought I was the only one." —C. S. Lewis

---

1. Where in your life have you been tempted to shrink back or walk with your head down? How can you remind yourself to "look up" and trust in God's plan for you?

2. Just as God always provided a friend for me in every new place, how has He shown His faithfulness in your life? Who has He placed in your path to encourage you—or who might He be calling you to encourage?

CHAPTER 7

RINGS & REDEMPTION, PART 2

Coming home from our anniversary trip, we slipped right back into the chaos of our WWF era—Worship, Work, and Family. Only now, it felt even harder. We were two ships passing in the night, caught up in the nonstop rhythm of church services, school activities, and a growing ministry that demanded everything from us. The good news? Our little church was thriving, and so was the Christian school we had started. I had left my full-time nursing job for a year to teach there, and watching our son and daughter fully immersed in school life made it all feel worth it.

Weekends were spent on the road, caravanning with other parents to away games, cheering on our kids from the stands, sharing meals, and swapping stories on long drives home. We were all in—100 percent invested in the school, the church, and the dream we had built together. And right in the middle of it all, we got the biggest surprise of our lives. A baby. (A lot more on that later.)

It was an exciting time. Fast, full, and fulfilling. But beneath the surface, something was unraveling.

We had been running on empty for too long, giving every ounce of ourselves to the church and the school. There was nothing left for us. I was exhausted—physically, mentally, spiritually. The warmth in our marriage had faded into cold indifference. When we did have time alone, conversations turned into arguments, so we just . . . stopped talking. Distance settled in, quiet but suffocating, until one day, Jason moved to the couch.

Years of unresolved conflict and neglect had finally caught up with us.

One evening, after yet another attempt to talk ended in frustration, I snapped. My voice cracked with exhaustion as I yelled, "It doesn't even feel like we're married!" And then, my eyes landed on our wedding bands, sitting untouched on the dresser. Without thinking, I grabbed them, walked out onto the patio, and with all the strength I could muster, I hurled them into the vast stretch of our backyard.

I stood there, frozen. Jason was right behind me, silent.

The rings were gone.

A strange mix of heartbreak and relief washed over me. Heartbreak, because I had watched my marriage slip away for months. Relief, because at least now, it felt over. No more wondering. No more fighting. No more trying. It was done.

What followed is a blur. Pain has a way of protecting you from the sharpest edges of memory. I went to counselors alone. We went together. We sought wisdom from pastors, mentors, anyone who might help. We took one last trip to the beach, hoping a change of scenery might fix what was broken. But we were too far gone, too raw, too empty.

I asked Jason to move out.

During that season, he resigned as pastor and took a job at a small wholesale distribution company that required him to travel. I threw myself into motherhood, filling every hour with my three children so there was no space left to think. I stopped answering calls. Stopped going out with friends. I was drowning in heartbreak but determined to stay busy enough not to feel it.

At night, when the house was quiet, I felt it.

My sister sent me a CD of songs to comfort me, and my best friend cried with me. A dear friend suggested I meet with a pastor. I had sat in front of so many counselors, mentors, and pastors by then that I wasn't sure it would make any difference. But something in me said to go.

I drove to the most beautiful church, unsure of what I would say, unsure if I even had the energy to speak. The pastor greeted me at the door with a warm smile. His curly gray hair framed kind blue eyes that held no judgment, only understanding. He sat across from me, nodding as I poured out my heart, listening without interrupting.

When I finally stopped, he leaned forward, and in the gentlest voice, he said the words my heart didn't know I needed to hear:

"Datha, let him go and let God bring him back."

That was it. One sentence.

But it was everything.

No more wondering. No more sleepless nights questioning where he was or what he was thinking. No more "why" or "what if." Just surrender. Just release.

And for the first time in months, I breathed.

I walked out of that church lighter, knowing—really knowing—that no matter what happened next, I was going to be okay.

---

1. Where in your life have you been holding on to something that God is asking you to release? How can you trust Him with the outcome, even when it feels uncertain?

2. In difficult seasons, it's easy to pour ourselves into busyness to avoid pain. How can you create space to truly seek God's voice and find peace in His presence?

CHAPTER 8

THE TREE

It was just a few days before Easter in 2019. Jason and I were settled into our living room on Vann Street, in the little fixer-upper we had poured two decades of love and labor into. The house sat on nearly two acres, giving us both the privacy we cherished and the endless yard work we dreaded—mowing, weeding, trimming trees. If Jason wasn't in the yard, he was inside working on yet another renovation. Year after year, we tackled a new project—a side deck, a screened-in porch that became my personal sanctuary, and finally, my dream master bathroom. We had converted a spare bedroom into a luxurious retreat: a massive two-bowl vanity with lighted mirrors, an expansive closet, and a waterfall shower. All that was missing was the soaker tub under the window, the final piece of a labor of love that had taken an entire year to complete.

That evening, at exactly 6:30 p.m., Jason and I had settled into our favorite spots—me on the couch, him in his recliner—watching my favorite game show. Jason humored me by playing along as I raced against the contestants, my competitive nature in full force as I tried to solve the puzzles before they did. I usually won.

The weather reports had warned of spring storms, but we'd heard it all before. As the wind began to howl outside, I decided to check the backyard. I stepped off the couch and made my way toward the kitchen. Just as I placed one foot inside the kitchen—BOOM! A deafening explosion shook the house, and the ceiling in front of me came crashing down.

I froze. My mind couldn't process what was happening. The only sound was my own screaming. When I finally stopped, I saw branches and debris in front of me, the shattered remains of our glass back door. I turned to look behind me—more limbs, more destruction. Jason was still in his recliner, wide-eyed, unmoving. Then I realized—Sophie.

"Stay in your room!" I screamed.

A massive tree had fallen on our house, its thick limbs blocking her bedroom door.

The sky outside had turned black, and rain was pouring through the gaping hole in our roof. Jason sprang into action, making his way to Sophie while I ran outside. The moment I saw the massive tree sprawled across our home, my heart clenched—but all I could do was whisper, over and over, "Thank you, Jesus. Thank you, Jesus."

Within minutes, fire trucks and power company crews arrived. The rain intensified, soaking everything inside. But we were alive. And in that moment, I had only one thought—save my pictures. Everything else was replaceable, but not those memories. We rushed to move photo albums, framed pictures, and cherished scrapbooks to a dry corner of the house. Then, we grabbed a few clothes, essentials, and drove to my parents' house for the night.

The next day, we returned to survey the damage. The sight was sobering—the towering tree that once stood beside our garage now lay sprawled across our roof, its weight crushing everything beneath it. We knew immediately: it would be a long time before we'd live here again—if ever.

Over the next few weeks, insurance adjusters came, packing crews salvaged what they could, and dear friends showed up with helping hands. Some helped us pack, and others donated to help with immediate needs. The outpouring of love was overwhelming. And through it all, I felt an unshakable peace.

I even went live on Facebook, standing in the wreckage of my home, testifying to the goodness of God. I could have been standing in the middle of my kitchen when the ceiling caved in. I could have been walking through that glass back door when the tree crushed it. Instead, I had taken only one step inside the kitchen. The difference between injury—or worse—and walking away with nothing but a small cut on my toe was a matter of seconds.

Later, I asked Jason why he hadn't jumped out of his chair immediately. He told me he had seen the limb pierce the roof behind me and knew it had to be the massive tree by the garage. He was strategizing—making a plan before he moved. Then he asked me why I hadn't run when the ceiling came down.

"I thought it was a tornado," I admitted. "I thought there was no need to run—just to pray."

Jason had been planning for the immediate. I had been praying for the immediate. And God? He had been preparing our future.

We never moved back to our little home on Vann Street. By the time we settled with the insurance company, nine months had passed. We met with contractors, but rebuilding would take too much time—time we weren't willing to invest. Instead, we found a new house, a new beginning. I called it The Haven on Mimosa. It was beautiful. It was peaceful. And it was where so many new dreams were birthed.

It was home.

1. Have you ever experienced an unexpected storm—whether literal or figurative—that changed the course of your life? How did you see God's protection and provision in the midst of it?

2. In difficult seasons, do you tend to focus on making a plan, or do you turn to prayer first? How can you learn to trust God more fully, knowing He is always preparing your future?

CHAPTER 9

MUSIC

It's always been there—music. It was a presence, a thread woven through every memory, every home, every car ride, and every church pew. It was the one constant in my ever-changing childhood, a source of comfort, joy, and belonging. No matter where we lived or how often we moved, I could always count on music.

My mother's love for music began when she was just a little girl. Her mother took her to a small Pentecostal church down the street, where the pastor's young wife invited her to sit beside her on the piano bench. With patient hands, she taught my mother her very first song, "Every Hour of Every Day." My Paw-Paw, seeing her growing passion, bought a towering upright piano for their home. And so, day after day, my mother sat before those ivory keys, playing that one song over and over and over. Aunt Bennie, their next-door neighbor, would stop by for coffee and conversation, dramatically lamenting, "Can't you make her stop playing that song?" But my mother was undeterred. She played it until she mastered it, and then she moved on. I'm sure Aunt Bennie was thrilled!

She learned more songs, refined her technique, and before long, she was playing for Sunday services at that little Pentecostal church.

On the other side of the South, in Georgia, my father and his twin brother were falling in love with music, too. Their home was filled with the twang of country melodies drifting from the radio. Inspired by their idols, they picked up guitars and taught themselves to play, their fingers tracing chords until they came alive with sound. Their talent didn't go unnoticed. A local talent scout discovered them, and soon, the brothers found themselves performing on live radio shows, their voices and guitars filling the airwaves.

My parents were a perfect pair—my father, a tall and striking young preacher with a rich, commanding voice, with a guitar in his arms, and my mother, a vivacious brown-eyed beauty with a quick wit and fingers that could play any song after hearing it just once. I imagine young women in the congregation sighing over my father while envying my mother, who not only had undeniable talent but a preacher husband to match.

Music was the heartbeat of my childhood. No matter where we lived, there was always a piano, a guitar, and a record player spinning melodies into the air. It was a free and ever-present source of joy, a gift my mother used to its fullest. With a limited budget but an unlimited love for music, she made it an essential part of our daily lives. Evenings often turned into family sing-alongs, my mother at the piano, patiently teaching us our parts. My little sister, Rynn, sang soprano, I carried the alto, and Daddy filled in with the tenor. Mom's harmonies were flawless, and sharp or flat notes were swiftly corrected. She encouraged us to listen closely to records, to find our favorite voices, to mimic them, and to develop a style of our own.

When I was ten, we moved to South Bend, Indiana, where my father took a new position as a pastor. Our rental house was small but nice, and our neighbors, Mrs. Holycross and her son, welcomed us with Tang (northern orange Kool-Aid) and cookies. They were extremely kind, and I can imagine probably curious about their brand-new southern neighbors! I still remember the day my sister accidentally put her hand through the glass front door. As my parents rushed her to the hospital, Mrs. Holycross kept me occupied at her house until they returned . . . with Tang and cookies.

South Bend was also where I met Dawn Deiter, the coolest girl I had ever seen. She had short blonde hair, wore earrings, and—most shockingly—jeans. In my small world, she was just the friend I needed, and we talked and played together every day at school. I was even invited to her birthday party!

That rental house was also where I first heard that voice—the one that changed everything. My mother had a new record spinning on the record player, and suddenly, a voice broke through, unlike anything I'd heard before. It was Reba. I froze, listening as her vocals soared—soft and sweet, yet powerful and commanding. I was captivated. Our home had been filled with the harmonies of The Rambos, a gospel trio my mother adored, and Reba was their daughter. She was young, fresh, and completely mesmerizing. Soon after, I got my hands on her solo album, *The Lady Is a Child*, and I spent hours lying on the floor, listening, memorizing, and mimicking every note.

While my mother encouraged us to find our voices, she was quietly discovering her own. After years of playing other people's songs, a dream had been stirring inside her—one of her own melodies, her own words. One day, she sat at the piano, notebook open, and began writing. The melodies in her mind found their way to her fingertips, and slowly, line by line, she brought her songs to life. I watched as she created something entirely her own—a world of music rich with meaning, and she invited us to be a part of it.

In 1980, when I was twelve, I stepped inside a recording studio in Nashville, Tennessee, for the first time. I watched in awe as my mother sat at the piano, playing her songs for a room full of studio musicians. They scribbled notes, created charts, and then—one by one—her songs came to life.

She recorded ten songs that day:

"A Light in the Harbor"
"If Your Eyes Are Dry"
"He Traded Life"
"His Love Brought Me Through"
"I Want To Be The One"
"Take Me To The Cross"
"His Strong Hand"
"He Ransomed Me"
"The Bride Wears The Name"
"Humming a Song"

The last one was extra special. She had written it about her grandmother, just for Rynn and me to sing. We each had a verse. But when the moment came, Rynn was too nervous to step up to the mic. So I took a deep breath, climbed onto a small stool in the dimly lit studio, and sang both verses. I wasn't afraid. I wasn't unsure. I was a twelve-year-old girl in a room full of professional musicians, and I felt like I belonged.

That confidence came from my parents. My mother had spent years preparing me at the piano, teaching me through her own example. And my father—every single day—had poured words of affirmation into my heart. You can do anything. I heard it so often that I believed it.

A few days later, we had a photo shoot for the album cover. My mother had bought us long, flowing dresses in a soft peach hue. Mine was covered in tiny white polka dots, with a square pilgrim collar and a sash that tied in the back. At a local park, my parents posed together while Rynn and I walked behind them, picking wildflowers.

Those days in the studio shaped me in ways I wouldn't fully understand until much later. I watched my mother step boldly into her dream—no longer just playing the songs of others but bringing her own music into the world. She had spent years filling our home with music, teaching us, encouraging us, and now, she was leading by example.

She never had to tell me to chase my dreams. She showed me how. She taught me that dreams aren't just wishes—they are built with time, faith, and relentless dedication.

Looking back, I realize that my mother didn't just give me music.

She gave me courage.

She gave me the belief that what you hold inside is worth bringing into the world.

---

1. How has God used a constant in your life—like music in this story—to bring you comfort, identity, or purpose?

2. What gifts or passions has God placed in you that you've been hesitant to step into? How can you take a step of faith toward them today?

CHAPTER 10

TAYLOR

It's her birthday today, and I picked out a present fitting for Taylor's twentieth. Something I knew she would like. A delicate gold necklace in the shape of a little jar with several tiny mustard seeds inside. It was on a little card that had a scripture verse. As I filled out a "Happy Birthday, Niece" card, I thought about the incredible young woman she had grown up to be. Taylor loves Jesus, is kind and thoughtful. She's mature in her faith, and some would call her an old soul. I giggled when she told me about one of her first dates with her current fiancé. They went to a downtown park to witness to people about Jesus. That's Taylor.

I was there at the hospital the day she came into the world. The waiting room was full, and finally it was my turn to go back and meet her. She was a big baby, weighing in at nine pounds. Her little arms appeared to have muscles, and her head was cone-shaped—too long in the birth canal. She had a headful of black curls and beautiful olive skin, which answered the question that had weighed heavily on our hearts.

It was about eight months before her birth that I walked up the stairs to a tiny apartment with my husband. His sister, Ginger, and her husband, Brian, waited inside. I knew what was to come, and I had a huge lump in my throat. I had been preparing myself, but no matter how much I prayed, I felt no peace. It's like knowing a tornado is coming and there is no way to hold it back. It's coming, so you better just hide in the basement, wait for it to pass, and be prepared for the aftermath.

Ginger had wanted us to be with her when she told her husband that there was a possibility that the baby she carried was not his. Even as I write this, I lose my breath and tears flow. How does a marriage survive this news? It doesn't. How could it? Infidelity in a marriage is not uncommon, and many marriages can be reconciled through counseling, therapy, and the hand of God. But this was different . . . a child had been created.

I knew from the moment that I found out about the pregnancy that Ginger would choose life. That her faith in God would sustain her and that her family would gather near and protect her. We would be fiercely protective. We believed that God would forgive her, love her, and wrap his arms around her. But what came next was the most incredible moment of reconciliation that I have ever witnessed in the tiny apartment we were all standing in.

As Ginger started to share her news with Brian, a heaviness engulfed the space we were in. I don't know how it happened, but the heaviness took us all to the floor, and we all lay there and wept. The pain was tangible, and my heart was hurting. We wept. For the longest time, there were no words, just tears. Somehow, we made our way to a sitting position.

Then Brian spoke.

I don't remember most of the words that came out of his mouth, or the exact details of the conversation. That's not really important anyway.

"Let's stay together, Let's work it out, Let me be this baby's dad." That's what I heard.

I witnessed the most powerful moment of forgiveness and reconciliation. It was a moment that changed me, that showed me the grace and love of God like I had never seen. That was over twenty years ago, and the moment still stays with me. At times when I've been hurt or wronged and I hang on to unforgiveness, not eager to let it go . . . I remember.

That moment in the apartment was one of those unexpected places—raw, painful, holy—where purpose began to be reclaimed. Where shattered dreams weren't the end of the story, but the soil for something new. It was a reminder to keep dreaming, even when the path takes a turn you never would've chosen.

---

1. When have you witnessed or experienced true forgiveness and reconciliation? How did it reveal God's grace in a deeper way?

2. Are there any areas in your life where you are holding onto unforgiveness? How can you invite God to help you release it and rebuild with His love?

CHAPTER 11

THE BAPTISM

I know how awful this sounds, but here goes. As a teenager, I swore—swore—that I would never marry a pastor. Ministry? No thanks. Church life? Hard pass. A quiet, predictable life away from all that? Yes, please.

Then I married a nice, non-pastor man. Well, more of a boy at eighteen. Perfect. Life was going according to plan. Until one day, that nice, non-pastor man/boy found Jesus, dedicated his life to the Lord, and decided we should start attending church. Not just casually—no, sir. He wanted us front and center, on the serve team, fully involved. Whoa, Nelly. Pump the brakes. I saw where this was headed.

So, like any rational woman avoiding a life of ministry, I got a weekend nursing job to make sure I was conveniently unavailable for church. It worked like a charm—until the day my husband made an announcement:

"I feel called to the ministry."

Excuse me? You feel called?? That's great, babe, but we didn't discuss me signing up for this! I was over here just living my life, and now you want to pastor?

But, being the supportive wife I am, I agreed to attend a few meetings with a trusted ministry advisor who was helping Jason transition into full-time ministry. I sat quietly, listening, observing, nodding along—until the moment came.

"Datha, how do you feel about this?"

The whole room turned to me, waiting for my response. I had a choice: I could lie and say, Oh, I'm just thrilled! or . . . I could be honest.

I went with honesty.

"I fully support my husband . . . but . . ." (I turned to Jason's sister, who was sitting across from me) "Can SHE be the pastor's wife?"

The room laughed. I did not. I was dead serious.

I had grown up in a pastor's home. I knew the expectations. And let's just say, I was not what people envisioned when they thought *pastor's wife*. I wasn't meek and mild. I wasn't a rule-follower. I wasn't graceful or perfectly put together. I was loud. I was fun. I was the wild one. And let's be real—I used the "S-word" way too much. How in the world was this going to work?

To make things even better, we lived in a small town where everyone knew Jason's past—his reckless teenage years, the parties, the late nights. And now, suddenly, we were Pastor Jason and his wife with a "before being saved" reputation. What could possibly go wrong?

Despite my skepticism, we embraced our roles, grew in our faith, and watched as our little church started growing too. One of the best moments was when I got to witness to a coworker, who then brought her family, who then brought her mother, Belinda—a classy, elegant woman who had never been to church but soon gave her life to Christ.

One Sunday, Belinda decided to get baptized. Glory, hallelujah! As the pastor's wife, I was thrilled to walk her through the process. I even reminded her: "Bring a towel and a change of clothes."

What I didn't do? Specify what kind of clothes she should wear for the baptism.

Sunday morning rolled around. The worship team and I were on stage, belting our hearts out, while my young husband stood in the baptistry—a small, homemade setup in the front of the church. The back doors swung open, and there came Belinda, striding down the center aisle like she was walking a runway in Maui.

She was wearing a full floral bathing suit. One-piece, mind you, but bold, bright, and topped off with a perfectly matching sarong.

I kept singing. My voice got higher. The tempo picked up. Everyone on stage was sweating.

Belinda floated down the aisle, looking like she was about to step onto a tropical cruise. My husband, standing in the water (pool? baptistry? Who even knew at this point?), turned an alarming shade of red.

I whispered under my breath, "Dear Jesus, please let her keep the sarong on."

She reached the front, gracefully climbed the steps, and then . . . time stood still.

She untied the sarong.

She let it fall.

And then she stepped into the water.

I don't know what my husband said. I don't think he knows what he said. But whatever it was, it was said fast—and then, boom, she was dunked, and it was over.

From that day forward, I never forgot to specify baptism attire again. In fact, for the next twenty years, every single person in our church knew exactly what to wear.

---

1. When has God led you into something you swore you'd never do, and how did it shape your faith?
2. How do you handle the tension between who you think you are and who God is calling you to be?

CHAPTER 12

MISS RICHLAND JUNIOR MISS

It was my senior year at Richland High, and I was thrilled to have built-in best friends—my twin cousins, Lesa and Lora. Their mom, Aunt Bennie, and my maw-maw were sisters, but you'd never know it. Maw-Maw was Pentecostal Holiness, all about modesty, and Aunt Bennie? She was short, round, wore stretchy knit pants, and bright red lipstick like it was war paint, and—unfortunately for my teenage eyes—slept naked. I discovered this traumatic fact when I stumbled into her one night on my way to the bathroom. Some things you can't unsee.

Despite their differences, both women loved to talk and laugh—though Aunt Bennie's laughter often came with a well-placed expletive for emphasis. She was fabulous. She once took the twins and me to Kmart and bought me a baby blue tube top, which I'm fairly certain gave Maw-Maw a mild stroke. And oh, could they cook! Huge, sprawling Southern feasts with fresh garden vegetables, golden cornbread, and the best dumplings you've ever tasted—every meal was a masterpiece, the kind that still makes my mouth water to this day.

Life with Lesa and Lora was full of adventure—camping trips, sleepovers in their king-sized waterbed (that once started leaking in the middle of the night and we woke to sleeping in a river), and impromptu concerts featuring Rita Coolidge and Captain & Tennille, complete with hairbrush microphones and enough dramatic flair to rival Broadway.

Aunt Bennie's husband, Uncle Ray, was just as colorful. He had a thick head of black hair and the eccentric charm of a man who knew how to enjoy life. He taught us poker using matchsticks, cheered when we won, and spent hours in his backyard workshop, hammering away at furniture while belting out whatever tune struck his fancy. The legend goes that once he was singing a gospel song and accidentally hit his hand with the hammer. He busted out an expletive and then kept on singing!

Senior year, the twins and I had the dream schedule—we were out of school by noon. Every day, we'd rush to Aunt Bennie's, where a full Southern meal awaited. We'd pile our plates high and plop down in front of the TV for *Days of Our Lives* and *Another World* before I'd head off to my job at a local daycare. That job was courtesy of Maw-Maw, who had more influence in town than the mayor. Hazel Maughon was a force, and I was about to find out just how much pull she really had.

One day, the school announced sign-ups for the Junior Miss pageant. I had never been in a pageant before, but something about it intrigued me—probably the idea of wearing a fancy dress and getting out of class. The competition included an interview, a talent portion, an evening gown round, and a group dance. I borrowed a stunning red gown from my cousin Tammy, my mom picked out my song and would accompany me on the piano, and I was ready to go.

Then came the first dance practice. We were told we'd be wearing pastel-colored leotards and matching tights for the group number. Cute, right? Wrong. Because somehow—probably through the

Holiness grapevine—Maw-Maw found out. And before I knew it, I saw her marching into the gym, beelining for the pageant director.

Within minutes, an announcement was made: "Ladies, we will now be adding flowy skirts over the leotards." To this day, I cackle at the mental image of Maw-maw sweetly but firmly informing the director that her granddaughter would not be prancing around in a skin-tight leotard. And the best part? The other girls were thrilled. Turns out, no one was excited about showcasing every curve and dimple in a one-piece spandex nightmare.

The night of the pageant, we twirled around the stage to "Girls Just Want to Have Fun"—flowy skirts billowing, modesty intact. Honestly, I'm shocked Maw-maw didn't insist we change the song to "I'll Fly Away" or "The Sweet By and By." If she had, I bet she could've pulled it off. People loved and respected her that much.

For my talent portion, I stepped onto the stage wearing my mom's long black coat, holding an umbrella above my head. She started playing the piano, and I began to sing Barry Manilow's "I Made It Through the Rain." At the chorus, I flung off the coat to reveal a sparkly dress (also borrowed, because we were working with a budget).

We dreamers have our ways
Of facing rainy days.

Looking at the lyrics now, nearly forty years later, I'm stunned. My mom, knowingly or prophetically, had chosen a song that would become the anthem of my life.

I didn't take home the Richland Junior Miss crown. That went to Miranda, who won over the judges with a passionate poem she recited about a dog named Spot. And hey, I get it . . . I'm a huge dog lover myself!

But I did get first runner-up. And when Miranda later declined the one-year scholarship to a local college, it was passed down to me. So in the end, I didn't win the title, but I won the prize.

And I did it in two borrowed dresses, with my mom at the piano, singing me straight into my future.

---

1. Who are the colorful characters in your own story—those who shaped you, challenged norms, or protected your dreams—and what impact have they had on the person you've become?

2. Think about a time when you didn't "win" the way you expected, but gained something even better. How did that experience prepare you for what came next in your journey?

CHAPTER 13

THE DAY GOD WINKED

Today was special—one of those days you never want to forget. Exactly one month into my writing journey, I attended my first writer's small group. I had been anticipating this day for weeks. It was in the home of a new friend, Anna, who has written several books.

I woke up early and settled into my usual morning routine—coffee, candle, worship music, journal in hand, curled up in my well-worn spot on the sofa (so well-worn that a blanket had to go beneath me to keep me from sinking). Then I saw it—my calendar, with WRITING CIRCLE written in my favorite Paper Mate Flair Medium. Excitement bubbled up again.

I got ready, made the forty-five-minute drive, and arrived ten minutes early—perfect. Still excited, I walked to the door, stepped inside . . . and cue Beethoven's Fifth Symphony—dum dum dum DUM.

The moment I entered Anna's beautiful and welcoming home, impostor syndrome tried to take a seat in my mind. *Datha, you've been writing for a whole month . . . you don't belong here. You're not really a writer. You're a fraud.*

Shut up, liar! I wanted to scream—but thankfully, I kept that part to myself. Instead, I was greeted warmly with a Southern hug from Anna, met a few people, was offered coffee, and found a cozy spot on an oversized cream sofa.

Then, I reached into my purse . . . no pen. The writer with no pen—fantastic. I found Anna and asked for one, and without hesitation, she handed me a Paper Mate Flair-medium. I wanted to look up and wink.

I settled back down, scanning the room as everyone found their places. My eyes landed on the oak coffee table, where a large book sat—*Lighthouses of North America*. The beautiful cover jolted my memory. Just a few days earlier, I had been on vacation, wandering through a little shop in the Bahamas, searching for a keepsake. Among the ocean waves, palm trees, and (oddly enough) paintings of swimming pigs, I had stopped at one print—a lighthouse. It drew me in. I don't own a single lighthouse anything, but I couldn't put it down. So I bought it. And now, here I was, staring at a lighthouse book on the coffee table.

I snapped a picture. I wanted to remember this moment forever—the day God gave me two winks, letting me know I was right where I belonged.

Settling in, I turned my attention to Anna as she began to share. Suddenly, two deer meandered into her backyard. Without thinking, I pointed and blurted out, "Deer!"—completely interrupting the hostess. I wanted to smack myself. But Anna just laughed graciously. "That's why I sat in this chair," she said, "so y'all would face the view."

I promised myself I wouldn't interrupt again, because I knew something good was coming. And it did.

The deer lingered. Birds of every color danced at the feeder outside the expansive windows. And then Anna introduced Amy.

Amy and I had spoken briefly when I arrived. She had bright eyes and a kind smile, and later, I noticed her unique and effortless style—flowy patchwork skirt, oversized sweater with textured brown stars, blue high-top combat boots, and gold seed bead earrings. But when she spoke, I was captivated. She shared her journey as an illustrator and author—the hard parts and the beautiful parts.

At one point, I found myself leaning in, elbows on my knees, fist under my chin, completely lost in her words. I scribbled notes furiously, but one line cut through everything else:

"Reaching for something beautiful is not a waste of time. We have a limited number of years . . . why would we not?"

When it was my turn to share, I repeated her words. And the tears came.

It always happens like that when I feel so completely loved by my Heavenly Father. The entire day felt like a big, tight hug. Like He picked me up, held me in His lap, looked at me adoringly, and placed His hands on my head as only a loving Father would.

The others kept talking, but all I heard was Him:

You're not too old. It's not too late. Your dreams matter. You are seen. Someone needs to read what you write. The journey you are on IS the destination.

To the woman who wonders if she belongs, if her dream is worth it—this is your reminder. God sees you. He is already in the places He is calling you to step into. And sometimes, He leaves little winks along the way just to remind you . . . You're right where you belong.

---

1. Have you ever felt out of place or unqualified in a space where God had clearly led you? How did He affirm your belonging and purpose in that moment?

2. What "God winks" or small confirmations have reminded you that you're on the right path—especially when self-doubt tried to take over?

CHAPTER 14

PEPPER

Years ago, I was visiting the home of a dear friend's son for their annual holiday tradition—Santa Claus visiting friends and family. Convincing my then twelve-year-old daughter to join me had been no small feat, but eventually, she agreed. As we mingled, I heard clawing sounds coming from the kitchen. Curious, I asked about it and learned it was a seven-month-old puppy kept in the washroom. The family had purchased her, but with a baby and a toddler to care for, they had little time or energy left for the puppy.

I asked to see her, and when they brought her out, my heart melted. She was a tiny ball of tangled hair, her eyes barely visible. Despite being told she was hyper, not potty trained, and had snapped at their toddler, something in me just knew she needed me, and I needed her.

I asked if I could take her home, but they refused, saying they had paid too much for her to give her away. Yet three weeks later, I received a call—they had decided to let her go, and she became ours.

When we brought her home, we quickly realized her "hyper" behavior was actually fear. She darted under tables, chairs, and beds, trembling. Treats were the only way we could coax her out, but if we tried to hold her, she'd frantically wiggle, desperate to escape. It was clear she had little experience with humans. Even her groomer suggested putting her on medication because of her anxiety.

But instead of resorting to medication, we chose patience. Every day, we coaxed her onto our laps, scratched her ears, rubbed her back, and gently reassured her. It took over a year of persistent kindness, but one day, she jumped into my lap on her own, eager for her ear scratch. My husband, watching in awe, exclaimed, "Look what love did!"

Pepper, now six years old, is unrecognizable from that frightened little puppy. She wakes me every morning with kisses, excitedly leading me to her food bowl with a prance and a glance back to make sure I'm following. Through Pepper, we've learned that love requires patience and persistence, and that brokenness can only be healed through consistent acts of kindness.

Her story reminds me of 1 Corinthians 13:4–7, which says, "Love is patient, love is kind. It does not envy, it does not boast, it is not proud. It does not dishonor others, it is not self-seeking, it is not easily angered, it keeps no record of wrongs. Love does not delight in evil but rejoices with the truth. It always protects, always trusts, always hopes, always perseveres."

Just as God's love transforms us, Pepper's journey taught us that love can overcome fear and heal even the deepest wounds. When we encounter others who may act out of hurt, we remember Pepper's story and the grace God shows us. With persistence and kindness, love truly has the power to redeem.

1. Can you think of someone in your life who, like Pepper, may be acting out of fear or hurt? How might God be inviting you to show them patient, persistent love?

2. Reflect on a time when someone's consistent kindness made a difference in your life. How did it help heal or shape you, and how can you offer that same kind of love to others?

CHAPTER 15

JESUS DISAPPEARED MY PHONE

What would happen if we laid down our phones to be more present and picked them up to do Good only?

A few weeks ago, my husband and I were up before dawn, excited to catch a flight to Fort Lauderdale for a much-anticipated cruise to Key West and the Bahamas. With our luggage packed and vacation mode activated, we backed out of the driveway—until I reached into my purse and felt . . . nothing. My phone was missing.

Cue the chaos.

We tore through the house like detectives on a high-stakes case. I retraced every step, flipped couch cushions, and even checked the fridge (because, at this point, anything was possible). I knew I had it in the kitchen—I had taken a picture of my calendar, just in case I needed to schedule any meetings. (Oh, the irony.)

Time was running out, and as I frantically searched the car one last time, I heard myself say something truly shocking:

"Should we try to move our flight?"

Excuse me?! Was I really willing to risk missing a VACATION because of my phone? That moment hit me like a ton of bricks. I turned to Jason and said, "Let's leave it."

Thirty minutes later, we rushed into the airport, made it through security (thank you, tiny Birmingham airport), and boarded our flight—me, phoneless for the first time in years.

What followed was six days of absolute freedom.

No notifications. No endless scrolling. No mindless distractions. And as I walked around the ship, sat by the pool, and took in the breathtaking views, I noticed something heartbreaking—everyone else was glued to their screens.

Heads down at dinner. Heads down at the pool. Heads down in the elevator. Heads down, missing everything around them.

And then it hit me—I had been one of them too.

Phones are useful, yes. But they're also a constant distraction, stealing moments we'll never get back. And after six days without one, I felt like I had been through a detox. When I finally picked my phone up again, scrolling through the negativity and drama on social media, I had one overwhelming thought:

I don't want to consume this garbage.

I prayed and asked God what I could do. His answer?

Use my phone to DO GOOD ONLY.

I want to use it to encourage, to celebrate others, to document blessings, to share Jesus. Maybe I'm just having a moment, but what if we all looked up more and used our phones to bring light instead of distraction?

Funny thing—just before my no-phone experience, I grabbed a sticker at my favorite coffee shop. It was a picture of Jesus, and instead of sticking it on my coffee cup (which would eventually be thrown away), I stuck it on the back of my phone.

Three days later, when my phone went missing and we finally gave up searching, I looked at Jason and laughed: "Jesus disappeared my phone."

---

1. How might your life look different if you were more present in the moment and used your phone only to encourage, uplift, or glorify God?

2. What are some intentional steps you can take this week to disconnect from distractions and reconnect with what truly matters—God, people, and purpose?

CHAPTER 16

GRIEF

Our businesses were thriving. I had received a huge promotion with my online health and wellness company, and we had opened two boutiques. With excitement and gratitude, we purchased a new home—a dream home in a neighborhood I had long adored. It had an expansive front porch, a sprawling lot, and endless potential. But it had been vacant for years and needed love—so much love. Right after Thanksgiving, we finally got the keys. We hired a contractor to remodel the kitchen and bathrooms, and Jason and Brian dove in alongside him, painting every wall with care. For months, we poured ourselves into that house, counting down the days until we could finally call it home.

Then, the day before our long-awaited move, tragedy struck.

At the time, we were living in a rental house thirty minutes from town, nestled on a beautiful piece of property overlooking the water. It was quiet, with only a few neighbors. That morning, I lingered in bed a little longer than usual while Sophie and Jason went about their morning routine. Our two pups, Petey and Pepper, were restless in their kennels, eager to start the day as they always did— side by side.

Then, frantic voices broke the morning stillness.

I jumped out of bed and ran to the window above the kitchen sink. My eyes weren't sharp without my glasses, but I didn't need them. I saw the small brown shape lying in the road. My heart knew before my mind caught up.

I ran outside and knelt beside him. Petey was gone.

He was Sophie's baby. Jason's loyal little companion while she was at school. And now, in an instant, he was taken from us. I knew it would be me who carried him inside, who wrapped his tiny body in his favorite blanket, who placed him gently in a small plastic tub. Me who made the solemn drive into town. We had never cremated a pet before, but when Jason stood in the yard, shovel in hand, we knew—we just couldn't bury him. Petey had been with us for three years and eight months, and in that time, he had become an important part of our family.

He had been Sophie's thirteenth birthday present. In July 2019, I took her out of town to celebrate, leaving Jason with one simple task: find a puppy—small, cute, preferably white and fluffy. Jason delivered . . . sort of.

Petey was small—tiny, in fact. The first time I saw him, I almost gasped. He weighed less than a pound, his head oversized for his tiny body, his bug-like eyes full of curiosity, and his enormous ears standing at attention. He was a strange little mix—half Chihuahua, half mystery—but we loved him instantly. And Petey loved us right back. Wherever we went, he went too. He was our shadow, our constant companion. Every afternoon, he rode with Jason to pick up Sophie from school, ears perked, tail wagging. He grew into his ears, his eyes, his awkward proportions and became the most adorable little thing. We took hundreds of photos, capturing every silly antic. We had loved many dogs in our lifetime, but none like Petey.

We wished for a million do-overs of that morning. Two years have passed since we lost him, and we still miss him terribly. But heartbreak has a way of multiplying.

Just before Thanksgiving 2023, grief came knocking again. Jason's father, Kenneth Warner Whitfield, suffered a stroke and left this earth at eighty-five years old. There was no doubt in our minds that when he met Jesus that day, he was welcomed with the words: "Well done, my good and faithful servant."

Kenneth was the embodiment of commitment and dedication. One of seven children, he grew up poor and left school in the sixth grade to work. When he was old enough, he joined the Navy, and upon returning, he married his sweetheart, Barbara Jane Thomas. They built a life together in a small three-bedroom, one-bath house on Clyburne Street, where they raised their four children. For nearly sixty-four years, they remained in that same home, their love and faith steadfast.

Jason, Kenneth's only son, had prepared a beautiful message for his father's funeral. We had spoken about it many times—about the words God had placed on his heart to honor the man who had meant so much to so many. But in a sad twist of events, he never got the chance to speak.

Losing his father so suddenly was devastating, but being unable to share his tribute deepened the wound. After the service, I found Jason in the hallway, his face etched with a grief I had never seen before. Friends who understood the weight of the moment surrounded him, praying as he stood in silence. It was then that we truly understood the meaning of the phrase pouring salt in a wound.

Two years have passed since Kenneth left us. If you've lost someone dear, you understand—grief is a strange companion.

Sometimes, it crushes you, stealing the air from your lungs. Other times, a memory will surface, bringing a smile, a laugh, a fleeting moment of warmth.

But grief never really ends. It walks beside us, reshaping itself over time, but never fully leaving.

Below is a summary of the tribute my husband wrote for his father. I thought it was fitting to include this tribute here. My prayer is that this chapter and tribute will help us all think about the power of legacy and examine our own lives.

November 28, 2023 by Jason Whitfield

On a day like this, it helps me to think about the qualities of Jesus. On the hardest days, that's what calms the soul.

Jesus was a teacher—His lessons shaped lives.

Jesus was forgiving—even to the ones who hurt Him.

Jesus was gentle—He welcomed children and cared for people with kindness.

Jesus showed self-control—steady in every storm.

Jesus was honest—He didn't just tell the truth, He was the Truth.

Jesus was prayerful—before every big step, He prayed.

Jesus was humble—He came not to be served, but to serve.

Jesus was loving—nobody was outside His reach.

Jesus was compassionate—He saw people's needs and He cared.

Jesus was obedient—always about His Father's work.

Now, those are the qualities of Jesus.

But maybe as I read through them, you noticed something.

They sound like somebody else we knew.

They sound like my dad.

All my life, he was my teacher. He didn't just tell me—he showed me. He let me get in the grease with him. I remember being barely tall enough to hold the handles of the tiller, and he walked right behind me, steadying my hands until I could plow the garden. He taught me about life too—responsibility, finishing what you start, never quitting. That was him.

People sometimes looked down on him because he wasn't highly educated. But he never held a grudge. Never carried bitterness. He was quick to forgive.

Nobody was more gentle. From holding babies to talking with children, he had that soft, steady way. He didn't raise his voice. He was quick to smile.

And self-control? That was my dad. He didn't lose his temper. He never yelled, not even when mom got upset—he just stayed calm.

My dad was honest. If he found a dollar in the parking lot, he'd try to find the owner. "Honest as the day is long" is about the truest thing you could say about him.

He loved to pray. As a child, he'd take my hand and lead me into the prayer room. As a man, I watched him come to church early, go straight to the altar, and pray. Whether at church or at the kitchen table, he prayed with his whole heart.

And he was humble. He always put others above himself.

He was loving. My dad didn't just say he loved—he showed it.

And his compassion—well, if he knew of a need, he was going to do something about it. He invited the lonely to dinner. He drove people to doctor's appointments, bought groceries, helped clean, and gave whatever he could. He just took care of people.

At the heart of it all, my dad was obedient to God. Even when money was tight, he still tithed, still gave to missions, still honored God. His life lined up with the Word, and he lived it.

That's a legacy worth leaving. Because when a man's life looks like Jesus, you can't help but be pointed back to the Savior.

A man's legacy isn't measured by what he had, but by the Christlike qualities he passed down.

And I'm grateful . . . I saw Jesus through my dad.

1. When you think about the people you've loved and lost, what Christlike qualities do you see reflected in their lives—and how can you carry those qualities forward?
2. If someone were to describe your legacy today, what parts of your life would point them back to Jesus?

CHAPTER 17

KINDNESS

"Be kind." We hear it all the time. It's on T-shirts, coffee mugs, and Instagram captions, usually in a cute font with a little heart. But let's be honest—sometimes it feels more like decor than a way of life. Real kindness, the kind that sticks with you forever, is rare. But when it happens, it's unforgettable.

I was about twelve, traveling with my family while my dad preached a series of revival services. One stop was a big church in Indianapolis. At the time, I was deep in my "awkward phase." Picture this: oversized glasses, unfortunate teeth, and the kind of confidence only a preteen with no concept of fashion can have. But the real tragedy? My hair.

You see, I desperately wanted bangs, but cutting my hair was not an option. So, I got creative. Every night, I'd stand in the bathroom, section off some hair at the front, wet it down, and carefully roll it into a pink foam curler. By morning, I'd unroll my "bang" (yes, singular), wet it again, and stretch it into what I believed was a stylish fringe. Spoiler: it was not. And yes, there are pictures. No, I don't know why my mother allowed this.

So there I was, strutting into church with my makeshift bang, when a girl named Ann took one look at me and said, "Want me to do your hair?" I was stunned. Was this an insult? A rescue mission? Either way, I mumbled, "Uh . . . yeah?"

Next thing I knew, she was dragging me to the church bathroom, which, to my surprise, doubled as a full-service beauty salon. From under the sink, she pulled an arsenal of tools—curling irons, hair sprays, and a giant bottle of Rave (the '80s MVP of hair products). She got to work, and when I emerged, I was a new person. My bang was gone, replaced by a glorious, Texas-sized '80s POOF.

Poof: the pinnacle of hairstyling excess—big, bold, and gravity-defying. Sky-high bangs, teased and sprayed within an inch of their lives, creating a voluminous wave that defied both nature and reason. The key ingredients? A comb, a can of Aqua Net or Rave hairspray, and a complete disregard for minimalism. It was the era of the bigger, the better, and the '80s poof was a crown of confidence for those who rocked it.

For the first time in my awkward, preteen existence, I felt cool. Ann could have laughed at me, whispered about my DIY disaster, or let me continue living in denial. But instead, she chose kindness. And I have never forgotten it.

Fast forward about twenty-five years. Now, I'm thirty-nine, exhausted, and running on caffeine and Jesus. My husband and I had started a Christian school, my kids were involved in everything, and we basically lived at the church. Wednesdays were the hardest. We'd leave early, have a tiny window at home in the afternoon, then rush back for Bible study and youth group.

Enter Tammy. Sweet, wonderful, saintly Tammy. One day, she approached me and said, "I want to help you on Wednesdays." Immediately, I said no. She had her own family, her own responsibilities. But Tammy wasn't taking no for an answer.

And so, every Wednesday for an entire year, Tammy showed up at my house. She cleaned. She cooked. She left dinner on the stove. I'd come home to a spotless house and a warm meal—two things I had no time or energy for. Because of her, that tiny window of time on Wednesdays wasn't a frantic blur. It was a moment to breathe. Instead of exhaustion, there was rest.

Ann and Tammy—two people, two completely different acts of kindness. One small, one massive. But both changed something in me.

Kindness isn't just a slogan or a hashtag. It's noticing. It's stepping in. It's making someone feel seen. And trust me—it's never forgotten.

Kindness is God's love in action. Jesus didn't just preach love—He lived it, stopping for the weary and lifting the broken. When we follow His lead, even the smallest act of kindness becomes a seed of His grace, planting hope in ways we may never see but heaven never forgets.

---

1. When was the last time someone's unexpected kindness made a lasting impact on you—and how can you pay that forward this week?

2. Is there someone in your life right now who needs to feel seen, supported, or uplifted by a simple act of kindness from you?

CHAPTER 18

DADDY

My daddy and his twin brother came into the world on December 12, 1944, born at home in the quiet countryside of Georgia. I can only imagine the shock and joy when two babies arrived instead of one—long before ultrasounds could prepare their parents for such a surprise. They were named Darrell and Harrell, and their resemblance was so uncanny that even their own mother and father struggled to tell them apart.

Johnny and Noie, their parents, were hardworking people who made their living in the cotton fields. My grandpa Johnny was a small man, only about 5'4", with dark hair, a deep complexion, and a quiet presence. He didn't say much, but he loved animals and was rarely seen without a cup of coffee in his hand. Grandma Noie, on the other hand, was his perfect opposite—full of life, laughter, and stories. She had a head full of curls, bright eyes, and a smile that could light up a room. She loved to talk, to laugh, and to have a good time. I'll never forget the trip I took with her and her best friend to New Orleans when I was seventeen. I was the driver, but they were the real adventurers, walking up and down Bourbon Street, pointing, laughing, and soaking in every moment.

My dad's childhood wasn't easy, but it was typical for those who grew up in the backwoods of Georgia. His parents worked hard all week, but on the weekends, their home transformed into something magical—a gathering place for music and fellowship. Friends and family would arrive with guitars, fiddles, and jars of moonshine, filling the night air with the sounds of country tunes and laughter. Shorty, Coyle, Willis, Woodford, Brother, Guynell, and Sarah were regulars at the Wilson house. My dad recalls that as the night stretched on, and the bottle passed around one too many times, the songs would shift. What began as country ballads often turned into old gospel hymns like "Kneel at the Cross."

It was in those late-night gatherings that my dad and his brother discovered their love for music. They would watch the guitar players' fingers move, waiting for their chance to grab an instrument when someone took a break. Their talent quickly became undeniable, and before long, they were known throughout the community. Their big break came when a man named Red Healan invited them to perform on WRFC in Athens, Georgia, the very station where some country legends got their start. They sang "Crazy Arms" by Willie Nelson, and I can only imagine how the girls in town swooned over the twin boys with rich voices and the talent to match. They were just teenagers, unaware that their lives were about to change forever.

One late afternoon, Uncle Bill and Aunt Dorothy arrived unexpectedly, driving an hour just to share some news. They had been born again at a little church in Athens, Georgia, and they couldn't wait to tell the family about Jesus. Oh, how I wish I could have been there to see that conversation unfold—to watch their excitement as they shared the gospel with a family that had never set foot in a church, never owned a Bible, never even known God in a personal way. Uncle Bill must have been persuasive because that very

Sunday, Grandpa Johnny loaded up the whole family and took them to church.

That little church on 151 Chattooga Avenue became the heart of their Sundays. They would pack a picnic lunch and spend the entire day there, soaking in the Word. Before long, the entire Wilson family was baptized in the Oconee River. And it was there, in those waters, that my daddy's life was forever changed. As a child, he had suffered from seizures after a terrible fall, but the moment he was filled with the Holy Spirit, he was completely healed. The trajectory of the Wilson family was rewritten that day.

Last year, my dad and his twin brother turned eighty. Family traveled from all over the country to Watkinsville, Georgia, for a three-day celebration. Twenty-five of us, along with their youngest sister, spent the days visiting places that had shaped their lives—old home places, schools, fields where they worked as teenagers, and cemeteries where loved ones rested. But the most sacred stop was the Oconee River, the very place where the Wilsons had been baptized so many years ago.

We made our way through the woods, some of us brave enough to walk the winding paths, others choosing to watch from the bridge above. When we reached the riverbank, my precious eighty-year-old father waded into the water alongside my sister's son, Brody. As Brody went under, we all began to sing. When he came up, he threw his fists in the air in victory, and there wasn't a dry eye on the shore.

I didn't think that moment could be topped—until the next day.

Our last stop was that little church on 151 Chattooga Avenue, which had long been converted into a single-family home. The plan was simple: drive by, take a few pictures, and hope we didn't startle the homeowners. But when I arrived first, I noticed a man standing outside.

I parked the car and got out, approaching him with a smile.

"Are you the homeowner?" I asked.

What happened next could only have been arranged by God.

"Yes," he said. "And actually, the house is for rent. I just finished showing it to someone."

I couldn't believe it. I explained the significance of the house—how it was once the church where my family found Jesus, how it was sacred ground to us. Just as I finished, the rest of the family arrived, walking up behind me, and without hesitation, the homeowner invited us all inside.

We stepped through the doors in awe, taking in the walls that once echoed with hymns and sermons. My daddy walked slowly, memories flooding his mind.

"This was the Sunday school room," he said.

"This was where the pews sat."

And then, he walked to the right corner of the room and placed his hand on the floor.

"This," he whispered, "is where the potbelly stove sat—the very spot where I lay down as a little boy and asked God to heal me and come into my life."

The presence of God was thick in that room, and we all stood in reverent silence. Then, my sister began to sing an old hymn by Bill Gaither, her voice full with emotion. One by one, we joined in, our voices rising together—just as they had all those years ago in that very place.

He touched me, oh, He touched me
And oh, the joy that floods my soul.

That trip to Georgia will forever be etched in my heart. I am overwhelmed with gratitude for Uncle Bill and Aunt Dorothy, whose simple act of sharing the gospel changed the course of our family forever. Because of their obedience, a legacy of faith was born in a humble little house at the end of a red dirt road in Georgia—a legacy that still echoes through generations.

---

1. Who in your family or community first shared the love of Jesus with you, and how has their obedience impacted your life?

2. What sacred places or moments in your story remind you of God's faithfulness—and how can you honor or share those memories with the next generation?

CHAPTER 19

THE HEALING

2023 was a tough year, to say the least. Grief had invaded our lives, along with sickness. Everyone knew about the grief—social media and texting spread the tragic news of the passing of loved ones, and friends and family kept in contact with sweet messages of comfort and support.

But the sickness? That we held close, telling only a few people.

As soon as we finished the big house remodel and moved into our new home, we were absolutely exhausted—like could-not-hold-our-heads-up exhaustion. We're definitely not spring chickens anymore, so we chalked it up to the toll of remodeling, packing, and moving. I took a few weeks off and noticed my energy returning, but Jason didn't. March turned to April, then April to May, and Jason was still exhausted—feeling awful and, quite frankly, with a mood to match.

Finally, in June, we both had doctor's appointments with blood work and several tests. We got some answers. Jason's diabetes was out of control, his blood pressure was high, and he had an infection. New medications were prescribed, and a continuous blood sugar monitor was highly recommended.

I felt some relief that we had answers, but I'd be lying if I said I wasn't angry. Angry that he had waited months before going to the doctor. And probably even angrier because my blood work showed that I was slap dab in the middle of menopause. Yippee. (If you know, you know.)

July arrived, and although Jason strictly followed his new medications and diet, he wasn't improving. His feet and legs began swelling.

July 4 was approaching, and we had been anticipating a trip to see my sister for months. All our children and my parents were headed to Kingwood, Texas, where we would all be together at my sister's home for the first time in years. She has a beautiful home with a resort-like backyard—a pool, hot tub, swings, tropical plants—a literal oasis in Texas. Plans were made, my brother-in-law had purchased the brisket, and we were all set to have the best time . . . but Jason was much too sick to travel.

I should have been the empathetic wife—kind, caring, "in sickness and in health"—but I wasn't. I was angry.

Months of sickness had robbed Jason of his ability to work, to think straight, to sleep, to participate in life—and now, to travel. I was angry at the sickness. Angry at him for delaying medical treatment for months. So, I left him at home, loaded up the car, and drove to Texas. And a few days later, on July 4, he ended up in the emergency room.

Reading this now, it sounds so cruel. But at the time, I was just so incredibly angry. And something else had begun to take root in my heart—something called bitterness.

I returned home, and things continued to decline. He could only stand for short periods, and his feet and legs were severely swollen. Sophie and I moved an old recliner from storage into the living room and plopped it right in the middle of the floor. Now, even my pretty living room was affected.

More doctors' appointments. More tests. Changes in medications. Still no answers.

For the first time in our marriage, I had to cut the grass because he was unable to. I pulled the riding lawnmower out of the garage, got a quick lesson on how to operate it, and off I went—for the first time ever. Two hours later, I could barely walk. I had put the pedal to the metal, hitting every hole and bump in our expansive two-acre yard. I spent the next few days soaking in the tub and applying Icy Hot. Lesson learned.

Summer turned into fall. Fall into winter. And still, no answers.

The nurse in me had researched and diagnosed—kidney failure? Heart failure? New meds? What could be the problem?

We were at a loss.

We were praying. Our family, our church—praying. It was the hardest experience—to watch my husband get sicker and sicker and be completely helpless. Our marriage was suffering. Our finances were suffering. Every day was a struggle. The sleepless nights were unbearable. It felt like we were stuck in time, just waiting for a healing that wasn't coming.

Every morning, we would sit in the living room, pray, and listen to worship music. "I'm Gonna Wait for You" became our anthem. But we were growing weary.

Then January came, and the swelling was worse than ever. He couldn't wear shoes, and the swelling had crept up the entirety of his legs, reaching his hips. By the end of January, his prayers had become desperate: *God, heal me or take me.*

Then, sometime during the last week of January, Jason was sitting in that old brown recliner, and I was walking into the kitchen. That's when my eyes landed on a bottle of virgin olive oil sitting on the counter by the stove. It had always been there, but that day, as I saw it, a memory came alive. It was as if I had been transported back in time.

I was six years old, standing beside my dad in a big 1970s Pontiac as he drove down a two-lane road in Topeka, Mississippi. There were towering pines on both sides of the road, and on the expansive dashboard sat a bottle of olive oil. I was with my dad—who pastored Ballard's Chapel—on our way to pray for someone who was sick.

At that exact moment, standing in my kitchen, I felt a nudge from the Holy Spirit.

"Pour the oil on his feet and legs."

Immediately, I grabbed a towel from the bathroom, walked back into the living room, and placed it under his legs, which rested on the recliner. I pulled a chair from the kitchen table and sat in front of him.

Jason looked at me, confused. "What are you doing?" he asked.

I muttered an answer while I poured the oil. Then, I felt another nudge.

Rub the oil in.

I didn't want to.

I didn't want to rub oil into his feet and legs.

I had let bitterness creep into my heart, and the last thing I wanted to do was care for the very person who had become the object of my resentment. I had allowed all my hurt, anger, and disappointment to rest on my husband's shoulders. I had let bitterness steal my joy and distort my perspective.

All my focus was on the negativity surrounding his sickness and the situation it had put us in.

But I obeyed that day.

And the next.

And the next.

For weeks, it became part of our morning routine—Jason sitting in the recliner, legs up, and me pouring oil and rubbing it in. And as I did, my perspective began to shift. As I surrendered my bitterness to Jesus, He replaced it with healing, joy, and peace.

What I had begrudgingly done at first became something I looked forward to.

And as the days passed, the swelling in his feet and legs began to diminish.

On February 20, it was completely gone.

My husband was healed.

A few days later, Jason stepped outside, gone longer than usual. When he finally walked back in, his arms shot up in triumph, fists pumping the air. "I did it—I changed the oil in the car!" His smile was radiant, and in that moment, what seemed like a simple task became a hard-won victory.

Walking through this season with my husband has changed me in ways I never expected. I see joy in the moments I once overlooked—the privilege of taking a walk together, laughing at nonsense, dreaming about the future. Simple things we had unknowingly let slip away, now cherished more than ever.

Sometime later, Jason was able to stand up in a local church and minister. God had given him a beautiful revelation of healing.

My hope and prayer is that you receive the healing you need and find hope in our story.

---

1. Have you allowed bitterness, resentment, or disappointment to take root in your heart during seasons of prolonged struggle—and what might God be inviting you to surrender in exchange for healing?

2. How have you seen God's faithfulness in the midst of unanswered prayers or painful waiting—and what small acts of obedience might He be asking of you right now?

CHAPTER 20

APRIL FOOLS'

So, April Fools' Day rolled around, and normally, I don't participate in the shenanigans. But on a whim, I decided to stir the pot
a little. I posted:

"It's finally time to spill the beans . . . after much thought and
reflection, we have officially decided! We found our dream home in
North Carolina and will be moving this summer!"

Since we are currently in North Carolina, I figured it might
be halfway believable. My husband is here for work, and I tagged
along to tootle around—a phrase I learned from my precious Maw-
Maw Hazel.

I cackled reading the responses. Some were heartfelt congrat-
ulations. Others were dramatic farewell messages. And then there
were my real ones—the folks who know me too well—immediately
calling me out with a solid "Yeah, right."

While I'm not actually leaving my hometown of thirty-seven
years, I have fallen in love with these tiny mountain towns. The foot-
hills of the Blue Ridge are magical. I've wandered through charming little places, exploring antique stores, museums, and parks. It

feels like another planet. Even the local Walmart is adorable . . . and I genuinely can't believe I just typed that.

Now, let's talk about yesterday. It started with a Zoom call with the most precious coaching client, followed by a Holy Ghost-inspired three-hour collaboration call for a new project. And where did this divine brainstorming take place? A hotel room inside Harrah's Casino. Oh yes. Jesus and I were making big plans right in the middle of neon lights and slot machines.

Walking through the casino lobby makes me feel so out of place. I've met several people, and let me tell you—no one seems thrilled to be here. Most people I talked to were just . . . bored. One guy even told me, "I come here all the time. I'm bored." Others are here to win big, and you can spot them instantly. And then there's a massive crowd of elderly folks zooming around on electric scooters. Not a lot of smiles. Maybe they're saving their joy for when they hit the jackpot?

I'm seriously considering taking my Bible to the lobby today and doing my study front and center. Just set up shop between the slot machines and see what happens.

But back to yesterday's real adventure. I stumbled upon a River Walk, where I had the most peaceful three-mile walk. One of my coaching clients told me that her "God Wink" is hearts—she sees them everywhere: in the clouds, on the ground, in nature. They're little reminders from God that He's near.

So, as we ended our call, I prayed, asking for my own God Wink. I wasn't sure what it should be, so I left it open-ended.

Y'ALL. Less than an hour later, I'm walking through the woods, glance up at this huge rock formation, and BAM—there it is. A heart. I about fell out. I snapped a picture and sent it straight to her. Of course God gave me her wink.

Now I'm on a mission to find my personal God Wink. Maybe balloons? Still deciding.

After my walk, I wandered into downtown Murphy, popping into little shops. I met Randy at the local art museum, a nonprofit run by volunteers. He writes books, moved here from Miami seven years ago, and was the sweetest. He even read me a few chapters of his book out loud right there in the museum. Then, he introduced me to Jane—who had the biggest hair I have ever seen—and she pointed me toward a local diner for lunch.

Now, when I walked in, I knew I was in the right place. The place was packed with elderly regulars and men in dirty work clothes. That's a good sign.

I ordered fried chicken livers, field peas, squash, potatoes, cornbread, and sweet tea. My total? $7.50. I about fainted.

And y'all—those field peas took me out. I haven't had field peas that good since Maw-Maw Hazel made them for me. Before I left, I went up to the register to give my compliments to the chef. Naturally, I expected a little old lady with a bun to be behind the magic.

Nope.

Shirley at the register pointed to a guy lugging a huge pot of green beans. Before I could say anything, he grumbled, "What's wrong?"

This man—who looked exactly like Gomer Pyle—had a white sailor hat on that said MOOSE. I was tickled. I told him his field peas were perfect, and he just gave me a quick nod and disappeared into the kitchen. A legend.

I loved the River Walk and diner experience so much that I decided to do the exact same thing today. Three-mile walk, then a big plate of food—balance, right?

But as soon as I pulled into the trail parking lot, I spotted a black cargo van with tinted windows. The only other car there. Textbook Do Not Enter the Woods Alone vibes.

So, I did what any responsible woman would do—I snapped a picture and sent it to my sister. If I went missing, this was the van to find.

A few minutes later, my sister texted back: "Did you get the license plate?"

Uh. No. But I did glance at it and remembered it had Florida plates.

Then came her scolding. "Have you learned nothing from Chris Janson?"

Not even thirty seconds later, I spotted a guy coming down the trail toward me. Tall, blond, surfer-dude type, with a huge dog off-leash. I knew it was his van.

So, I pretended to take a picture of a wooden bridge—just in case I disappeared, there'd be evidence.

The guy walked past, his blond locks waving in the wind. I'm sure he was just as terrified of me—random lady standing there suspiciously with her phone out. We both survived.

After my walk, I was hot, sweaty, and looking rough, but I knew Shirley and Moose wouldn't mind. So, I marched straight into the diner.

Today was Thursday—Turkey and Dressing Day.

I went in exited because I love homemade turkey and corn-bread dressing!

Moose made his a little different . . . made with white bread instead of cornbread. Not what this southern gal was accustomed to . . . my taste buds were shocked. . . . Moose was full of surprises!

I was hyped. But y'all . . . I have bad news. The dressing? Tragic.

I was devastated. I wanted to slip them Maw-Maw Hazel's dressing recipe, but I didn't want to be that person. So, I just took my heartbreak and left.

All in all, yesterday and today were adventures, and I loved every second. So tomorrow who knows . . . eyes open for my God Wink, another hiking trail, a little antique store, and maybe a Bible study in the casino lobby. Let's see what happens.

1. How can you stay open to God's presence and joy in the unexpected, even in places or moments that seem ordinary or out of place?

2. What's one simple adventure or small joy you've recently overlooked—and how might God be inviting you to slow down and notice His "God Winks" today?

CHAPTER 21

THE FALL

It was several years ago, mid-January, and I vaguely remember hearing about extremely cold temps before I went to bed that night, but when Pepper woke me up at 6 a.m. for her morning potty break, it was the last thing on my mind. I quickly threw on a lounge set, slipped into my Ugg slippers, grabbed her collar and leash, and opened the front door. The cold hit me instantly, so I reached for my Columbia jacket, tossed it on, and stepped outside.

The chill was biting, and I pulled the hood over my head as I walked a few feet to the brick steps of my front porch. But the moment my right foot touched the first step, I started to slide. I knew immediately it was ice, but there was no stopping it. My feet flew into the air, and I bounced down all eight steps, trying in vain to grab the handrail. I landed flat on my back, Pepper's leash beneath me, my hood still over my head.

Pain screamed from everywhere—my legs, ankles, hips, and the back of my head. My first instinct was to get up, but I couldn't. I lay there, stunned, then cautiously wiggled my fingers and toes—thankfully, they moved. Then I heard it: loud moaning. It was me.

I don't know how long I lay there on the cold sidewalk. At some point, I began calling for Jason. The front door was open; only the glass storm door stood between me and the warmth of my home. I called and called, but he didn't come. So I stopped, and just . . . lay there.

Thoughts raced through my mind.

"It's a weather day—no school. No neighborhood kids walking by to flag down like a stranded mountain woman."

"My body feels warm . . . wonder how long this jacket will keep me from turning into a human popsicle?"

And then, because the brain does what it wants in a crisis, I remembered a scene from *The Revenant*. You know the one—Leonardo DiCaprio is being chased by hostile Native Americans, galloping through snowy wilderness. He ends up launching himself off a cliff, crashes into a tree, and lands in a snowbank. His horse dies (RIP), and in a move that haunts me to this day, Leo slices that thing open and climbs inside like a sleeping bag from a horror movie. Disgusting, but effective. I lay there on the ice, thinking: "Well, if Leo can survive subzero temps in a dead horse, surely I can make it a few more minutes in my Uggs and Columbia jacket."

Right about then, Pepper gave me a look. Not concern. Not sympathy. Just judgment. Like, "This is so embarrassing. You're a mess."

Eventually, the front door creaked open, and out popped Jason's head. "What are you doing?" he asked, as casually as if I were sunbathing in the front yard.

"I fell down the stairs!" I hollered.

To my horror, he stepped out further—for a better look, mind you—wearing nothing but boxer briefs. In fifteen-degree weather. On an icy porch.

"STOP! Do NOT come down these stairs!" I shouted. "It's solid ice! I think I've broken everything!"

He disappeared back inside to call 911 and put on clothes.

To this day, I have no clue how I did it, but somehow I managed to crawl my way back up those frozen steps and fall onto the living room couch. Jason was seconds away from calling 911. Maybe it was the threat of flashing lights and nosy neighbors watching from behind their blinds, or maybe it was genuine concern for the safety of the people who'd try to rescue me—but somehow I pushed through.

Miraculously, nothing was broken. My body was bruised, scraped, and sore for days. I still carry a dent in the back of my left leg and a deep aversion to those front steps. It took months before I could go down them again—and when I finally did, I moved slowly, carefully, one deliberate step at a time.

As I lay in bed those first few days, I found myself reflecting on other falls. As a child, I fell while roller-skating and landed on glass—stitches and a scar on my hand. I once tripped and embedded a rock in my leg. As a teenager, I fractured a pinky finger when a swing broke beneath me. My fingers were laced in the chains of the swing when it broke. I'll never forget the time I hit my pinky toe so hard on the recliner that I cried real tears—while trying to rush Jade to a doctor's appointment. When we arrived at her appointment, the pediatrician sent me to get an X-ray . . . broken toe.

You probably have your own memories of falls and injuries. Scars and stories that come flooding back when you least expect them. And while those experiences leave marks—on our bodies, on our pride—they rarely stop us. We still walk down stairs. We still skate, swing, and run. We fall . . . and we get back up.

Maybe you're not carrying scars on your body—but you have them on your heart. The kind no one sees. From grief, heartbreak, betrayal, or disappointment. Life knocked you down and left you cold on the sidewalk of your soul.

But friend—hear this: you're still here.

You've gotten back up more times than you can count. You may limp a little now, or move more slowly than before, but you're still moving. Still living. Still loving. And that's something to be proud of.

Scars may tell our story—but they're also signs of survival, strength, and healing.

---

1. What scars—physical or emotional—do you carry, and what do they reveal about your strength and resilience?
2. Can you remember a time when you fell—literally or figuratively—and how grace or grit helped you rise again?

CHAPTER 22

COFFEE SHOPS & GOD'S GOODNESS

Oh, how I wish you were here with me right now. I'm sitting outside the most charming little coffee shop in Carrollton, Georgia, and it's one of those moments that feels too perfect to keep to myself. The weather is soft and gentle—overcast with a breeze that whispers peace. I'm nestled under a grand old oak tree in the middle of a sweet little town square, surrounded by the soft hum of friendly conversations at nearby tables. The birds are literally singing, and I swear I'm living in a Hallmark movie.

I ordered my go-to—vanilla latte with oat milk—and y'all, it came in the most darling robin's egg blue ceramic cup with a matching saucer. An actual cup. This must be what heaven feels like. A lady just walked by and said, "Your coffee smells amazing," and I thought, *Yes ma'am, it does. And so does this moment.*

It's May first, and we close on our house in twenty-three days. Yesterday, we got a twenty-five-page inspection report full of surprises. Things like a foundation check and—get this—an attic inspection. Apparently, our attic was "too hot." It's Alabama in the spring. It was over eighty degrees. Shouldn't it be hot? I mean, doesn't heat rise? I'm pretty sure I've never known anyone to casually hang out in their attic, but I'm telling myself to just breathe and trust. We'll do the free inspection, they'll probably recommend insulation or a fan, and it'll be okay. Right?

Meanwhile, we don't have our next home lined up, haven't packed a single box, and my husband just started a new job that has him traveling Monday through Friday. That leaves me, our two-story home, a full basement, and a looming moving sale. I keep picturing myself in my gold Birkenstock wedges, a boutique top, and a tool belt, trying to DIY all the inspection fixes. Maybe I'll recruit some of my most fashionable friends to help—pure chaos, but with lots of coffee and laughter.

By all accounts, I should be spiraling. But I'm not.

Instead, I'm here, fully present, sipping from a ceramic cup and soaking in beauty. I've learned that peace isn't found in perfect circumstances—it's found in the presence of Jesus. I'm in my Joy & Peace era, and let me tell you, it didn't come easily. It came through growth, hard-fought trust, and a deepening relationship with the One who holds it all.

Spending time with Jesus has become my non-negotiable. Every morning, no matter where I am, I start the day the same way—coffee brewing, candle lit, worship music playing, and my prayer journal open. I sit with Him. I talk to Him. I expect Him.

That's been the key: expecting His goodness.

Each morning I whisper, "God, what are You going to do today?" And somehow, in the middle of the mess, He always shows up—sometimes in big ways, sometimes in tiny, quiet ones. A kind word. A surprise blessing. A friend who calls at just the right time. And the more I look for Him, the more I find Him.

Life will always come with circumstances—relationship struggles, money worries, health concerns, house sales—but those things don't have to steal our joy or peace. We don't walk alone.

So friend, wherever you are, whatever you're facing, sit with Jesus. Make space for Him. Expect His goodness.

Because even when life feels chaotic, He's still writing beautiful, sacred moments—just like this one.

---

1. What is one way you can create space in your daily routine to sit with Jesus and expect His goodness, even in the middle of uncertainty?

2. How have you seen God show up in small or surprising ways recently—and what does that reveal about His presence in your everyday life?

CHAPTER 23

THE HURT

I just left the most beautiful meeting with a real-life editor—yes, a real one! She was everything I could have hoped for: gracious, brilliant, warm, and incredibly kind. We sat down together and talked about the chapters I've been pouring my heart into, and while I followed most of what she said (thank you, Jesus, for those writing groups and the retreat that gave me some vocabulary), my heart is still pounding.

I sent her some of my work.

Now I'm in that sacred in-between moment—after the vulnerability, before the feedback—and honestly, I'm feeling a little lightheaded. The "what-ifs" are dancing around in my mind like shadows. What if it's not good? What if I missed the mark? What if she doesn't get it? The enemy loves to play in this space of vulnerability, doesn't he?

So I did the most logical thing. I ran to my happy place—a coffee shop—and I'm sipping on a perfectly crafted Toffee Nut and Praline Hot Latte (half sweet, of course), nestled in a real ceramic mug. There's a delicate little heart floating in the foam, which feels like God whispering, "I'm here, too." The café is alive with soft indie music and the hum of chatter. I look around and smile. I was just about to type "I'm the oldest person here," but the sweetest elderly couple walked in, hand in hand, and now I just feel peace. God has a funny way of reminding us we're never alone.

Yesterday, though? Yesterday was hard. Like, gut-punch kind of hard.

It's taken me a full twenty-four hours to begin peeling back the layers of emotion I've carried. You see, someone intentionally did something to hurt me. Not a stranger. An adult. A peer. Someone who knew what their action would do—and did it anyway.

It wasn't petty or small. It was a decision that carried weight. A decision that could have changed everything for the better—but instead, it left a wound. My initial response was a tidal wave: panic, dread, hurt, anger, sadness. The kind of sadness that settles into your bones. The kind that whispers, "They could have chosen differently." But they didn't.

So I called my husband, hoping he'd say something comforting—but really, he just reminded me of what I already knew: "It's going to be okay."

Still, I had to sit with it. I had to feel the feelings—not rush past them, not numb them, not cover them up with spiritual clichés. Just feel.

And then came the hard question, the one I didn't want to ask: "Datha, what amazing thing are you going to learn from this?"

That question felt too raw at first. Too soon. It stung. My emotions wanted justice. They wanted validation. They wanted to call my best friends and hear them say, "Tell me who did it—I'll handle it." You know, the ride-or-dies who would slash metaphorical tires for you in a heartbeat.

But deep in my spirit, I knew I had a choice.

I could either rehearse the offense or redeem the pain.

So, I asked again.

"What amazing thing am I going to learn from this?"

And I answered it.

I want to be kinder.

Not just surface-level nice, but deep, intentional, grace-filled kindness.

I want to understand—really understand—how my actions affect others. I want to carry awareness into every interaction, to leave people better, softer, more seen.

I want to be more generous. More mindful. I want my words to heal, not hurt. I want to be a safe place for others. I want to give love without demanding it back. I want to listen better and love more freely.

I want to become a woman who chooses kindness—even when it's not returned. Even when it's hard. Even when someone else chooses cruelty.

Because that's who Jesus is.

That's who He calls me to be.

Romans 12:21 says, "Do not be overcome by evil, but overcome evil with good."

And Philippians 2:3 gently reminds me, "Do nothing out of selfish ambition or vain conceit. Rather, in humility value others above yourselves."

Kindness, real kindness, is rooted in humility. And sometimes, it's only born through heartbreak.

Yes, I thought I was already kind. (Laughing at myself here, because doesn't God always show us we still have room to grow?) But now—I want to be kinder still.

If you live long enough, you'll meet the adult bullies. The unexpected betrayals. The sharp words. The closed doors. But each time, you're given a choice:

You can harden . . .

Or you can humble.

You can lash out . . .

Or you can lean in—to Jesus, to healing, to purpose.

And if you're brave, you can ask yourself the question: "What amazing thing am I going to learn from this?"

And then . . . let Him teach you.

---

1. When have you been tempted to respond from your pain rather than your purpose—and how can you choose kindness instead?

2. What is God trying to teach you through this disappointment, and how can you grow from it rather than grow bitter?

CHAPTER 24

CHILDREN

I have three children. Three wonderful, amazing, perfect children, and I'm sure you do too!

They like to do this thing whenever they're all together (which sadly doesn't happen as often as I'd like). I always want a picture, and they reluctantly stand side by side to make this momma happy. My three adult children each hold up their pointer finger, signifying that they are #1 in my eyes. I laughingly snap the photo and remind them that I love them all equally.

Jordan Bo is my firstborn. In sixth grade, he decided to go by Bo instead of Jordan, which confused the entire family who had always called him Jordan. To this day, everyone pre-sixth grade still calls him Jordan, everyone post-sixth grade calls him Bo, and a few compromise with Jordan Bo. It definitely makes things interesting!

Bo is now an associate pastor at Triumph Church in Vicksburg, Mississippi, and is married to Chelsea. God was exceedingly kind to bless him with a beautiful, talented, and godly wife. As a bonus, they even share the same birthday—so he'll never forget hers.

Together, Jordan and Chelsea gave me my first grandchild on January 6, 2014. He was absolute perfection and completely captured my heart. If you're a grandmother, you understand. If you're not, I can't explain it—grandmotherhood is something you have to experience to truly know. I cried and cried when I had to leave Vicksburg after his birth, knowing I wouldn't be there every day to hold him.

That precious boy also gave me my grandmother name. I was supposed to be "Honey," but one day "Detah" came out of his little mouth—and, as every grandmother knows, whatever that first grandbaby calls you, that's what you are for life! I have friends with all kinds of names—No-No, Tetah, Gella, Zaza—but mine stuck as Detah.

Raylan Bo is now ten years old and has a remarkable love for Jesus for someone so young. He collects Bibles, devotions, and studies, and he loves attending church and even writing sermons. For his sixth birthday, cousin Michael built him a pulpit, and he's preached me some mighty fine sermons since then! Beyond his sermons, he loves to laugh. We make up silly songs and stories together, and he ends up rolling on the floor in laughter. Raylan is also a Civil War buff—his knowledge amazes me. Honestly, he has taught me so much—mainly how to approach Jesus with everything I am.

Then there's his little sister, Layla Grace. Layla is four, a mixture of brilliance and wildness. She's beautiful, sassy, loud, brave, and incredibly funny! Napping is not in her nature; she's far too busy with talking and toys. Last summer, I took her and Raylan to Splash Adventure, a waterpark near me. Barely three years old, she tackled the waterslides with fearless enthusiasm. She would come off the slide, her little body shaking with excitement, and shout, "Do it again!"—over and over. She went down at least fifty times that day, just as thrilled the last time as the first. As loud as she is, she's equally sweet—running straight into my arms when I visit. I adore her. She has taught me how to live life with gusto and give it my all.

My secondborn, Jade Brookley, was the easiest pregnancy and easiest birth—and she's carried that same gentle and easy spirit into adulthood. She rarely misbehaved, happily played with dolls and crafts, and decided in third grade that she would be a teacher. She never considered anything else. It was a perfect fit.

On the day she graduated from the University of Alabama at Birmingham, her high school sweetheart, Jeremy, dropped to one knee while she was still in her green gown and proposed. Of course, she said yes! I had the incredible privilege of watching Jeremy grow into a godly man who now loves and leads his family so beautifully.

Christmas 2021 brought the surprise of my life. As we were opening gifts, I was handed a wrapped frame. In my mind, I thought, *There's no way I'm putting a picture of Ali the dog on my mantel.* But when I opened it, it wasn't Ali—it was an ultrasound picture! I was shocked. We had no idea they had been planning for a baby. Seven months later, Theodore "Teddy" Whit arrived—the cutest bundle of joy. I fell in love all over again. Teddy has beautiful blue eyes, long curly hair, and the best laugh. He loves Ms. Rachel, chicken nuggets, and stealing your drink. He is a first-class guzzler . . . and he is not picky, but I think his momma's Diet Coke is his favorite. Recently, he started a new hobby . . . collecting bottle caps at the local park. He will dig in the dirt for hours searching for the perfect one! Teddy reminds me daily that wonder is all around us if we'll only take the time to see it.

Just a few months ago, Teddy became a big brother when Benjamin "Benny" Wilson was born. His middle name came from my daddy, his great-grandpa, and Daddy reminds us of that daily. Benny loves his bottle, loves being held, and is bringing us fresh joy with all his little firsts.

Finally, my thirdborn—and my unexpected surprise baby— Sophie Brynn. She completed our family in a way I didn't know was possible. Jordan was seventeen and Jade was thirteen when she was born, and she shook everything up. When she was a child, we attended her daily "shows"—dance, art, singing, acting—always with paid tickets for entrance. She kept us entertained, laughing nonstop, and kept me completely worn out! Sophie has grown into a beautiful and responsible adult, always mature beyond her years. Watching her pursue every dream in her heart has been pure joy.

Over the years, friends have come to me with parenting questions—everything from handling difficult situations to managing disrespect. I'm no expert, but when I look at my children, I see amazing human beings who make the world a better place. I hope I had something to do with that. Looking back, I know we made mistakes as parents—but one thing I know we got right: we taught them about Jesus. We made Him the center of our family, took them to church, and lived out faith as an example in front of them. When life got messy, we ran to Jesus instead of away from Him.

---

1. When you look at the personalities, paths, and stories of your children or the young people you love, what has God taught you about Himself through them?

2. In what ways has your role as a parent or mentor shaped your faith—challenged it, strengthened it, or shown you what truly matters?

CHAPTER 25

MEXICO

It was 2020—peak pandemic—and while the world was slowing down, my network marketing business was speeding up. I hit the top rank! That little holy nudge I felt back in 2014? Turned out to be the nudge of the century. Everyone was stuck at home, scrolling their phones, and suddenly very interested in boosting their immune systems. And guess who had the supplements. 💁

Our team was in full-blown momentum mode—rocking, rolling, growing like wildfire. After six years and four months of consistent work, I hit the elite rank of DIAMOND—cue the confetti, commission checks, and a luxury trip to MEXICO!

Now, quick shout-out to the network marketing world: When it's done right? It's beautiful. When it's done wrong? Oof. It can be rough. I've seen both. But for me? It was mostly beauty—beautiful people, beautiful growth, beautiful breakthroughs. Customers who trusted me with their health, teammates who linked arms and built big dreams with me, and the unexpected friendships formed along the way.

Now, back to Mexico . . .

I earned a trip to the Banyan Tree Mayakoba—a beachfront slice of heaven in Riviera Maya. Think: private villas, candlelit dinners, jungle paths, and monkeys just lounging on marble floors in the lobby like they own the place. Literal monkeys. It was a luxury resort meets *National Geographic*.

We checked in and were immediately whisked away for the most romantic part of the trip: a COVID test. The contrast was hilarious—straight from paradise into a bleach-scented medical room where a man in scrubs came at me with a cotton swab the size of a drumstick. I did a little *Matrix* move to dodge the full jab, but my husband, Jason? He leaned straight into it like a warrior . . . and left with a nosebleed.

Thankfully, we both tested negative and were carted off to our private villa. And y'all—it was dreamy. Every morning, I sat there soaking it all in. Literally. I mean, who gets to wake up in a luxury villa and think, "Wow. God really brought me here."

So, on Day One, I decided to immerse myself in the luxury experience. Our bathroom had these giant sliding doors that opened to a private courtyard—with a massive outdoor tub surrounded by stone walls and little candle cubbies built in. I turned on the hot water, slipped in, leaned my head back, and let the sunshine and ocean breeze wash over me. Pure magic.

Until . . .

"Hola, Señorita."

EXCUSE ME?! Eyes flew open. Arms crisscrossed over my chest. And there she was—a kind, smiling woman, clearly here for "bath service."

Jason stood at the door shrugging like, "I told her no room service . . . but maybe she heard 'my wife is in the bath and would like some service.'"

And service I got! For the next ten minutes, this sweet woman lit all the candles, brought fresh towels, laid out a robe and slippers, and topped it off by sprinkling flower petals into my bathwater—while I sat there trying to be modest in a giant stone tub. Best (and weirdest) bathroom service of my life.

A few days later, I set off down a jungle path for a massage—still slightly traumatized from "The Tub Incident" and a little on edge due to rumors I'd heard about Mexican massages being "different." I didn't know what "different" meant, but I had theories. 👀

I was greeted by Claudia—sweet as pie and full of grace. She spoke a little English and made me feel totally at ease. First, she seated me in a cozy chair, placed my feet in a warm basin, poured herbal tea, and began a gentle foot massage. *Ohhhh,* I thought, *this is the "different" part!*

Then came the full-body massage—pure bliss. At one point, I'm pretty sure Claudia was actually on the table, straddling my back like a professional sumo wrestler of tension. My knots never stood a chance.

Afterward, I floated off the table and went to grab my flip-flops . . . only to find men's flip-flops sitting by the door.

Cue internal freak-out:

Wait . . . were these here the whole time?

Was a man in here?

Was it NOT Claudia on my back?!

I pointed in panic. Claudia looked equally confused. "Yes, your shoes," she said.

Then, in a sudden flash of realization, I looked closer . . .

They were Jason's. I had worn his flip-flops to the spa.

Mortified, I slid on the giant brown sandals, mumbled a thank-you, and practically ran back to my villa.

So yeah—2020 gave me a promotion, a pandemic, and a paradise I'll never forget. From flower petals in the bath to borrowed flip-flops, it was wild, holy, and hilarious.

But more than that, it was a reminder: when you follow God's nudge, even the unexpected becomes unforgettable.

---

1. What "God nudge" have you been sensing—and what's holding you back from trusting it?
2. Can you look back on a moment that felt awkward or uncertain and now see God's hand in it?

CHAPTER 26

CAMO

The dogs had me up at 5:30 a.m., so I've had a couple of hours to sit with my cup of coffee and Jesus. I felt the nudge to just sit. No notebook, no devotional, no Bible.

No agenda. No noise. Just Him and me.

Time slipped by, and in the stillness of my quiet home, peace came flooding in. He didn't speak in a booming voice. There was no tug on my heart. Just peace. In the silence, with morning light stretching through the window, I felt a sudden urge to walk.

I headed to my bedroom and opened the T-shirt and yoga pants drawer—you know the one. Right on top were the full-compression yoga shorts with pockets that Sophie had thrown in the garage sale pile. I'd rescued them a few days ago—almost didn't. They're army green—ugly, honestly, and not my color. 😄 I rummaged for a shirt and spotted one—green with big block letters on the front. The only green one in the drawer. Threw it on. Walked to the closet, looked at the three hats on the shelf, and thought, "Why not go full theme?" Grabbed the camo hat.

I scooped up my toddler dog—elder dog couldn't even make it around the block yesterday, bless her . . . I had to CARRY her around the block. Not doing that again . . .

So Pacey and I were heading outside, and something shifted. I felt like I was on a mission.

Then I caught my reflection in the full-length mirror. And it hit me.

I've been in a battle. Not with bullets or bombs.

A spiritual battle—for my soul.

The soul—your mind, will, emotions.

I've been surrounded by uncertainty, hurt, and loss. And just when I was at my lowest . . . the enemy whispered:

"You're not valuable. No one cares. You're worthless."

And I won't lie—it hurt. A punch to the gut when I was already down.

Everything in me wanted to react. But God said, "Be silent."

And in that silence . . . He showed me something.

Looking at myself in the mirror, dressed head to toe in army green with a camo hat, I saw more than clothes. I saw truth.

My shirt? IDENTITY.

My hat? JESUS.

Acts 17:28 – "For in him we live and move and have our being. . . . We are his offspring."

I. Am. HIS.

Simple as that.

He is the reason I rise.

He's the reason I move forward in purpose.

He is my passion.

He says I'm valuable.

He says I have a hope and a future.

He's working it ALL out for my good.

He is FOR me.

He fights my battles.

And can I just be honest?

There've been moments—whole seasons—where I doubted that.

I've cried on the kitchen floor. I've sat in the car longer than I needed to because I didn't want to go inside and face anything. I've hidden behind busy schedules and fake smiles and "I'm fine" when I absolutely wasn't.

But still—God showed up.

Not always loud. Not always obvious.

Sometimes in a sunrise.

Sometimes in a word from a friend.

Sometimes in a song that played at the exact moment I needed it.

And sometimes, like today, in a camo outfit and a mirror.

He is always speaking.

Sometimes we just need to be still enough to hear.

So I'll keep going.

Keep writing.

Keep encouraging.

Keep praising.

Keep dancing.

Keep thanking.

Keep loving.

Keep serving.

Just—keep going.

I'm five chapters away from finishing my first book in the hardest season of my life!

That sentence right there? I never thought I'd say it.

I've walked through fear, fought back doubt, wrestled with comparison, and still I'm here—typing, praying, hoping this encourages just one heart.

And if it does, it's worth it.

I'm standing here as living proof:

YOU CAN DO THIS.

Whatever "THIS" is.

Start the business.

Write the book.

Go back to school.

End the toxic relationship.

Say yes to the next thing God puts on your heart.

You don't have to have it all figured out. You just have to trust the One who already does.

I've even started thinking about the next book.

Working title maybe . . .

"In the Middle of the Hard, Messy, Painful, Uncertain, Devil-Thought-He-Had-Me Season . . . I MADE IT. And So Can You—Ten Steps to Overcoming Anything With Jesus, Coffee, Great Friends, Gratitude, and Joy."

(Maybe a little long.) 😄

But seriously . . .

You're gonna make it, Sis.

Not because you're strong enough on your own.

But because the One who lives in you?

He's undefeated.

The battle may be fierce.

The tears may fall.

The enemy may shout louder.

But God never loses. And He never leaves.

So today, if you feel weary . . .

If you're holding on by a thread . . .

If the voice of the enemy has been loud in your ears . . .

Pause. Breathe. Listen.

And know this:

You are loved.

You are chosen.

You are seen.

You are equipped.

And you are never, ever alone.

---

1. What lies has the enemy whispered to you lately, and what truth does God want to speak over those lies today?

2. In what areas of your life do you need to "just keep going," trusting that God is fighting your battles even when you can't see it?

CHAPTER 27

GIRLS' TRIP

Truthfully, it's been years since I've taken one like this. Sure—I've done retreats, conferences, family getaways. But a true, no-agenda, laugh-til-you-cry, sleep-til-you-wake, snacks-on-snacks, makeup-free, extra-salty-air kind of girls' trip? Not in forever.

You know the kind I mean—at least, this is my kind: no rigid plans, just belly laughs, long mornings, bottomless coffee, and the freedom to be exactly who you are with people who love you for it.

We met up in Mobile, Alabama—home to one of my dearest friends of twenty-five years . . . Kim. She moved here over a year ago, and I miss her so much. It was the perfect reason for several of us to gather . . . me, Kim P, Donna, Kim, Chrystal, and Leah.

This year, my mom and my mother-in-law came along, and honestly, it made everything sweeter. I'm at the age now where I want to make every memory with them. They are polar opposites—one is a walking comedy show, the other a quiet observer. You can probably guess which one's mine.

We hit the road with full hearts and a packed van, but before we'd even cleared the city limits, it was already time for a bathroom break. Over the years, I've conducted some serious bathroom reconnaissance (thanks to traumatic experiences in gas station stalls that shall never be spoken of). So I now have a short list of approved stops. First choice: Love's Travel Center.

As I browsed the coffee section, I exchanged a quick, kind hello with an older gentleman. Enter: Charlotte—my beautiful, unpredictable, and wildly entertaining mother. That's all you need to know to know something's about to happen.

While I was adding a little hazelnut to my coffee, I could hear the friendly chatter between my mom and the gentleman. As he reached for a coffee lid, the entire dispenser crashed to the floor. Flustered, he bent down to gather them up just as Mom leaned in to help.

"That's just like a man," she said with a grin.

Without missing a beat, he shot back, "That's what happens when I get around a pretty woman."

I made a full sprint to the door without so much as a glance behind me.

The laughter didn't stop all the way to Mobile.

The days have blurred together in the best way: lazy pool floats, snack breaks, casual conversations that somehow turn into sacred ones, and music debates (Mom is not a fan of my playlist). At one point, she walked past my speaker, gave it a death glare, and declared, "Alexia, play Bee Gees." We couldn't stop laughing. Later, she got sunscreen in her eyes, and Kim P, being the ever-helpful one, decided to rinse her with a bottle of water. What followed looked like a waterboarding scene from a spy movie.

Then there was dinner at Kravers, where the gumbo will make you "slap your grandma." There was so much laughter around that table that I'm sure the patrons thought we were drinking. . . . but all we had was sweet tea. I was physically hurting from laughter! It all centered around a conversation that I want to share so desperately, but if I do, my mother-in-law will disown me completely.

There's been nonstop laughter, yes—but also holy moments. And that's exactly what happens when beautiful friendships collide with our beautiful Jesus.

Yesterday was one of those days. The kind you don't forget.

This morning, I sat by the pool—just me, my journal, and the hush of a new day. Kim P was across the way with her own journal but had stepped inside for a coffee refill. Time seemed to pause. In that quiet, I poured out my thoughts to the Lord. Dreams, prayers, questions—some answered, some not.

And then Donna stepped outside, coffee in hand. No rush. No noise. Just presence. She sat beside me. And right then, the birds began to sing. One in particular, perched right above us, began repeating the same melody over and over.

Donna smiled, looked up, and said,

"Sing it, birdy."

And I kid you not—the bird answered. Rhythmically. Clearly. Like a voice from heaven:

"It's here—it's here—it's here."

In that moment, I felt the Lord whisper,

"This is a holy interruption. Don't miss it."

Friend, I don't know what you're waiting for . . .

Breakthrough?

Clarity?

Healing?

Peace?

Permission to dream again?

But I know this—

God knows exactly how to meet you in the stillness.

He knows the weight of every question you carry.

And He knows how to confirm what you don't even know how to ask.

That bird's melody wasn't random.

It was divine confirmation.

The season you've been waiting for? It's here.

The breakthrough you thought would never come? It's coming.

The shift you've been sensing in your spirit? You're standing in it.

> See, I am doing a new thing!
>   Now it springs up; do you not perceive it?
> I am making a way in the wilderness
>   and streams in the wasteland.
>   —Isaiah 43:19

And just when I thought the day couldn't get any more sacred, God surprised us again.

After the birdsong and soul journaling, we packed for the beach. One of my closest friends, Leah, drove four hours just to spend the day with us. It was beautiful—staring at the waves, talking about life, laughing, letting the sea wash over the noise of the world.

Later that evening, back at the house, everyone got ready to go out for dinner. Leah was going to grab a quick shower before heading home—her four-hour drive ahead of her. I decided to stay behind so I could soak up every last minute with her.

The others were standing by the door, about to leave, when suddenly the bathroom door swung open.

Out comes Leah—soaking wet, wrapped in a towel, water dripping down her legs—and she says,

"I was in the shower, and I didn't want y'all to leave without praying for me. Can y'all pray?"

Without hesitation, we surrounded her, laid hands on her, and heaven touched earth in that room.

Tears streamed down my face then—and they are again now.

Because Leah didn't care about how she looked.

She didn't worry about timing.

She didn't think she had to get it together first.

She just knew she didn't want to miss her moment.

And friend, that's the heart of it.

You don't have to clean yourself up to come to Jesus.

You don't need the right clothes, or a fancy prayer, or the perfect timing.

You don't need to have your act together.

You just need a willing heart.

Leah came soaked, wrapped in a towel, with her hair dripping and her heart wide open.

And Jesus met her right there.

That's grace. That's love. That's Jesus.

He's not looking for perfect. He's looking for present.

Not polished, just honest.

Not rehearsed, just real.

So come as you are.

Come with the questions, the ache, the doubt.

Come with the towel still wrapped around your uncertainty.

Come with the mascara running and the broken pieces.

Because when you come, He meets you.

And He makes it holy.

So if you've been waiting for a sign to turn back, to lean in, to open your heart again . . .

This is it.

It's here.

He's here.

And He's waiting—just for you.

1. Where in your own life might God be inviting you to pause and notice His "holy interruptions"?

2. What breakthrough or blessing have you been waiting on . . . and are you willing to come to Him just as you are, unashamed to receive it?

CHAPTER 28

THE BOUTIQUE

Somewhere between a dream and a dash of insanity, I opened a brick-and-mortar boutique in my little community. I dove in headfirst, doing all the things—including learning how to run a boutique with absolutely zero experience. I figured I loved beautiful things and I loved people—what could possibly go wrong?

Well, I quickly found out that boutique ownership was about so much more than curating cute outfits and loving on customers. It was everything in between that stretched me: the inventory systems, the marketing, the finances, the constant juggling. It was hard. But in the midst of the learning curve, something beautiful happened.

I met incredible people—customers who became dear friends. It was pure joy to see Monica, Susan, Delta, Kendra, Latoya, Candie, Shelley, and so many others walk through the door. And my small but mighty team? We had the absolute best time together. We shared laughter, dreams, a whole lot of hard work, and some hilarious moments we'll never forget.

Before we ever opened the doors, I had a massive custom sign made to hang behind the register. It read:

"God can do anything, you know—far more than you could ever imagine or guess or request in your wildest dreams" (Ephesians 3:20 MSG).

If I had to choose a life verse, that would be it. I've clung to it since 2014. It wasn't just a pretty sign—it sparked meaningful conversations and reminded me daily of why I started.

In those early months, something else caught my attention. I'd often hear women speak harshly about themselves while standing in front of the dressing room mirror:

"I can't wear this—my knees are fat."

"My elbows are ugly."

And on and on.

One evening, after a long day of overhearing these self-criticisms, something stirred in my heart. I thought, *What if I could gather these women together and remind them who they are in Christ? What if I could help them see themselves through His eyes?*

That's when it hit me—I looked up at the sign behind the register, and just like that, the name came: Wildest Dreams Women's Conference.

The idea was born right there in the boutique and came to life just a few months later.

Thanks to the incredible support of our community, we launched the first conference in 2021. And in 2026, we'll celebrate FIVE YEARS of the Wildest Dreams Women's Conference!

While the conference is still going strong, my little boutique closed after almost three beautiful years. It was bittersweet. I adored my community of shoppers, but the financial weight was heavy. We were just surviving from one holiday to the next, and the debt kept piling up. Eventually, the stress began to feel unbearable. We made the hard decision to close.

But sometimes I wonder—maybe the whole boutique journey, with all its joy and all its struggle, existed just to birth that one

God-inspired idea. And if that's the case, then yes . . . it was all worth it.

A social media caption recently stopped me in my tracks called "Three Things You Should Never Wear After 50." As a former boutique owner and a woman proudly in her fifties, I couldn't scroll past. Especially since my little boutique catered to women's fashion. A stunning woman gave a quick class on flattering fashion choices for the more "mature" woman. Good advice, sure—but that catchy title stirred something deeper in me.

It got me thinking about what we really need to stop wearing— the things that burden our souls, not just our closets.

In hopes that one of my former customers—or any woman who struggles with what they wear or how they look—might pick up this book, here is a little advice from me on what not to wear.

The Weight of Other People's Opinions

Girl, if they're not paying your bills or walking in your calling, their opinion doesn't get to dress you. You're not here to win a popularity contest—you're here to glorify God. "Am I now trying to win the approval of human beings, or of God?" (Galatians 1:10). Smile, nod, and keep strutting in your purpose.

Guilt from the Past

That outfit is out of style and no longer fits. Jesus already took care of it on the cross—so why are you still trying to wear it? "There is now no condemnation for those who are in Christ Jesus" (Romans 8:1). Toss that guilt in the donation bin and replace it with grace, gratitude, and maybe a little glitter if you're feeling extra.

The Pressure to Prove Yourself

Sis, the only thing you need to prove is that God is faithful—and you do that just by living fully and freely in Him. You don't have to strive, hustle, or perform. You just need to show up as the masterpiece He created.

So What Should We Wear Instead?

Joy. Wisdom. Peace.

Maybe distressed denim shorts and a floppy beach hat, because God didn't say we couldn't enjoy the sunshine! But above all, let's walk in the unshakable confidence that comes from knowing exactly who we are in Christ. We are chosen, loved, redeemed, and free. No matter what season you're in—whether you're soaking up rays or weathering a storm—your identity in Him never changes. And that's where true beauty and boldness begin.

---

1. What "outfit" have you been wearing: Other people's opinions, guilt from the past, or pressure to prove yourself. What is it time to lay down once and for all?
2. If you dressed yourself today in joy, wisdom, and peace, how might that change the way you see yourself and how you show up in the world?

CHAPTER 29

MELVIN

I was standing in a coffee shop in Hanceville (because apparently, my life revolves around coffee shops) with my very own personal therapist, Leah. Yep, you heard that right. God does stuff like that for me. I'm almost certain He looked down one day, smiled, and thought, "I like this girl. She's brave, tenacious, and just a tad crazy. She needs her own therapist." And so, into my life walked Leah.

Now, Leah doesn't look like your typical clinical therapist. She's got wild, curly hair, a nose ring, and more than a few tattoos. And I absolutely LOVE HER GUTS! (That's a favorite Leah quote, by the way.) She's one of the smartest women I know—and she loves Jesus with her whole heart.

We had met up for coffee and, like always, were deep in a great conversation. Then I said one sentence that would change everything:

"I think I want a life coach."

Now, let me let you in on a little secret: I had no clue what a life coach actually did. I just knew I had a lot to figure out, and maybe they could help. Without missing a beat, Leah said, "I know a guy."

Honest to God—that's exactly what she said. Then she gave me his number.

A few weeks later, I found myself sitting across from Melvin Airhart at Panera Bread. I had sweet-talked my husband into coming with me (he's used to my adventures), and I could just see the wheels turning in his head: "What is she dragging me into this time?"

To be honest, I don't remember much about that first meeting—what we talked about or even what convinced us—but when we stood to leave, we had hired a life coach.

In those early sessions with Coach Mel, we'd sit across from him at his big cherrywood boardroom table, coffee in hand, soaking up wisdom. And oh, did the wisdom flow. Through stories from his home state of Louisiana, life lessons, punchy one-liners, word meanings, sermons, and historical references—every session felt rich and meaningful.

Afterwards, Jason and I would grab lunch—usually Rock N Roll Sushi or Jason's Deli—and talk about everything Coach Mel had shared. Tuesdays quickly became one of our favorite days. It was a season of exponential growth.

Week after week, we showed up. And Coach Mel challenged us—spiritually, mentally, emotionally. Eventually, on March 20, 2021, he and his lovely wife, Cherry, came to our home and presented us with our Life Coaching Certification certificates.

When I look back on that season, I'm overwhelmed by God's goodness. We were completely changed—forever impacted by Coach Mel. And I can't help but think about all the heavenly puzzle pieces that had to come together to make it happen.

It reminds me of one of my favorite quotes by John Piper: "God is always doing 10,000 things in your life, and you may be aware of three of them."

If I hadn't said yes to Plexus . . .

I wouldn't have gone to that meeting at Blount Springs Chapel in Hayden, Alabama, on April 22, 2017 . . .

I wouldn't have met Leah . . .

I wouldn't have uttered the words, "I think I want a life coach" . . .

I wouldn't have heard, "I know a guy" . . .

I wouldn't have met Coach Melvin . . .

And you wouldn't be holding this book in your hands.

Melvin was the first person who looked me in the eyes and said, "Datha, you have a book in you."

I replied, "There are already so many books out there that people can read."

And he simply said,

"But no one has read yours."

---

1. Looking back, what seemingly small decision or unexpected moment became a divine setup, and how can you see now that God was orchestrating details behind the scenes long before you realized it?

2. Who has spoken life-giving words over you or seen potential in you before you saw it yourself, and how did their belief shape the way you view your calling today?

CHAPTER 30

CHARLOTTE

It's Friday, and I'm sitting in the lobby of a hotel in Charlotte, North Carolina. It's beautiful—soaring thirty-foot ceilings, floor-to-ceiling windows, and a color palette of greens and blues woven through the carpets and textured walls. Cherrywood furnishings add the perfect touch. Whoever designed this place knew what they were doing. Despite the ambiance and the generous free breakfast bar, my attention is elsewhere—it's the constant chatter from the tables around me.

I can't help myself. My family says I'm nosey, but I prefer interested.

To my left, two men in athletic wear are deep in conversation—probably in town for work. In front of me, a mother of four is buzzing around, making sure each child has what they need, filling plates, and asking questions. A man in a SALT LIFE shirt sits alone, glued to his phone, and an elderly couple nearby sips coffee and chats softly.

Each morning this week has started here. I've gotten a few sideways looks as I've made my hotel "specialty coffee" at the waffle bar.

Adding whipped cream and a drizzle of caramel—better than a coffee shop, if you ask me. The gym's nice too, but today I'm skipping the elliptical to sit and write about this week.

This is my first time in Charlotte. Naturally, I turned to TripAdvisor, and the Billy Graham Library was the top recommendation. As we drove into town, I noticed we were on Billy Graham Parkway and was telling my husband about the Library when—no kidding—we passed a gated entrance marked "Billy Graham Evangelistic Association." The gates were closed, but the lush landscaping and colorful flowers were beautiful. Jason slowed down, and right then, the sprinklers turned on—drenching our car. Without missing a beat, he said, "We've been baptized by Billy Graham!" We laughed. And yes, I know he was a full-immersion kind of preacher—me too—but it was a funny moment. Later, we realized our hotel sits right behind the Library. I joked about hiking through the woods to get there. Jason wasn't impressed with that idea.

The next morning, instead of exploring the city, I opted for a pool day. The heat was brutal—nearing one hundred degrees. I found a shady spot and reached for my book. A petite woman with a woven fedora and fabulous sunglasses approached. Her stack of bracelets caught my eye—my kind of girl. She sat at the only available umbrella table nearby, and a quick "hello" turned into hours of easy, fun conversation. We found we had so much in common, both in Charlotte for the week with our husbands working. As we were packing up, she asked, "What are you doing tomorrow?" and just like that, we made plans.

The next day, we explored the city together—boutiques, gift shops, lunch in the most charming old house (shout-out to 300 East), and a drive through historic neighborhoods. We ended the day at A Thousand Hills coffee shop, the only acceptable option when it's ninety-seven degrees. I prayed the air conditioning would be powerful, and thankfully, it was. We sank into a sofa and talked for hours while I sipped a lavender oat milk latte. I now have a new friend in Pennsylvania, and I'm grateful.

Back in the lobby now, breakfast is wrapping up, and it's almost time to pack up and head back to Alabama. People have come and gone, and I can't help but wonder about their stories. Jason joked that I should start a podcast interviewing hotel guests in the lobby. Honestly? That sounds amazing.

One thing is certain—we all have a story. A wonderful, beautiful, sometimes painful, often surprising story. You have a story, and it needs to be told. Maybe you don't dream of writing a book or standing on a stage, but what about your family? Have you ever stood in front of an old headstone, weathered by time, and wondered who that person really was? What did they live through? What did they love?

Stories are powerful. They connect us, inspire us, and reveal God's faithfulness. Someone needs your story—not in a grand way, but in your way. Just start. One word. One sentence. Someone is waiting.

---

1. If someone were to stumble across your story years from now, what would you want them to know about your life, your faith, and what mattered most to you?

2. What's one small step you could take this week to begin sharing your story-whether with your family, a friend, or even just your journal?

THE MAGNOLIA

You may have noticed the image of a magnolia scattered through-out these chapters. I chose the magnolia as a little tribute to Mississippi, to what's shaped me—my roots, my home state, the place where childhood memories were made and where Reno Street holds the fondest ones.

I was born in Jackson and spent parts of my life in Jayess, Brookhaven, Clinton, and Richland. My mama was born in Moss Point, my grandmother was from Seminary, and my son and his family are planted in Vicksburg. Mississippi isn't just where I'm from—it's the background music of my whole life. No matter where I've lived, I've always found myself saying, "I'm from Mississippi."

So the magnolia just fit; the symbolism can't be ignored.

Magnolias are beautiful, yes, but they're not delicate. They have thick petals, deep roots, and a way of standing through storms. They bloom big and bold, but they're also stubborn survivors.

And let's be real. . . . magnolias are a little messy.

They drop leaves the size of dinner plates.

They shed petals like confetti.

They'll have your yard looking like it needs a clean-up crew.

But they're still marvelous even when they have fallen.

Honestly? Same goes for life in the middle. It's not tidy. It's not always polished. Things fall. Things shift. Things change. And somehow, we're still here, still showing up, still blooming, still becoming.

So the magnolia became my symbol.

My ode to Mississippi.

My reminder of strength, Southern beauty, and grace that grows best when it's rooted deep.

And maybe this magnolia is also a hint of what's still to come, because the more I learn about this middle season, the more I realize there's another story taking shape . . . another layer of growth . . . another chapter waiting just past the next bloom.

But that's for the next book.

For now, the magnolia stands here—soft, strong, a little messy, and absolutely marvelous.

Just like the middle.

Just like Mississippi.

Just like me.

EPILOGUE

It's 5:30 in the morning, and I'm sitting in an empty living room on Red Leaf Lane. The house feels hollow, every sound echoing off bare walls. I had to make do with what's left—my old camping rocking chair from the garage, a large white ceramic mug from the last two on the counter, and a paint-splattered step stool from the kitchen to hold my coffee.

Before I settled in, I slipped into our dark bedroom. Jason stirred, his voice low, "Are you getting up?" I whispered back just as softly. It felt like a holy moment, and holy moments should be handled gently. I pulled my big, white, fluffy blanket from the corner of the room—one I rarely use—and brought it with me.

I opened the blinds, wrapped myself fully in the blanket, and lowered into the chair with a view of the front yard. The room was still, except for the soft tap of Pacey's little paws on the hardwood. He settled at my feet, warm and close. Outside, the first hint of sunlight pushed past the trees.

Epilogue

This is our last morning here. When we bought this house almost three years ago, we thought it was our forever home—a place to grow old together before the kids moved us into some retirement home. But it wasn't to be. That truth stings, even though I know deep down this is the right decision.

We've faced so much here—sickness, anxiety, menopause, financial loss, business failure, hard transitions, and even death. Some days the blows came so fast that Jason and I would just look at each other and laugh in disbelief. Surely this can't all be real? I'd ask myself, What's the lesson? What is God showing me? What will this pain produce?

Last night, I walked the dogs one final time through this neighborhood. As we rounded the bend, I looked up—and there it was. A double rainbow stretched across the sky, vibrant and unmistakable. It stopped me in my tracks. I've always known rainbows to be God's reminder of His promise, His faithfulness after the storm. But a double rainbow? It felt like His way of saying, Not only am I keeping My promises, I am multiplying them. It was a whisper of abundance, of blessing beyond what I can see right now. A message for this next chapter: I am with you, and I will do more than you've asked or imagined.

This morning, wrapped in my blanket, I realize why it's so significant. The blanket is called a Minky—a gift I never would have bought for myself. It's so luxuriously soft, I've always kept it draped over a chair, almost too "special" to use. But today, I've pulled it around me completely—like a cape—and I can feel the warmth sinking in.

That's what He has done for me here. He has wrapped me—intentionally, completely, without gaps. In every trial, He covered me. In every loss, He sheltered me. When the sharp edges of life cut deep, He softened them with His presence. He became my warmth, my safety, my rest.

Now, as the sun rises and floods the room with light, I see it all clearly—His goodness that never failed us here, His provision at every turn, the miracles I didn't deserve but desperately needed. I see the healing of body and mind, the dreams born in this place, the relationships formed, the breakthroughs we never could have orchestrated on our own.

Packing this house has been brutal. Jason was out of town, came home sick, and was diagnosed with COVID. Days later, I had it too. We were so sick we could barely stand, but still had to keep moving—packing boxes, lifting furniture, loading trucks, collapsing on the floor. Friends and family offered to help, but we couldn't risk exposing them. Somehow, we did it. All week, I kept repeating that trendy phrase, "I can do hard things."

But this morning, I know the truth.

I can't do hard things.

He can. And His Spirit in me did every single one of them.

That's the lesson. That's the amazing thing I've learned through every season here—sickness, anxiety, menopause, financial loss, business failure, transitions, even death. I can walk through all of it and survive because of Him. That's the difference. He did it. He does it.

So, sister—if I can make it, you can too. Look to Jesus. Cry out to Him. Trust Him. He will never leave you or forsake you. Open your Bible. Spend time with Him. See Him in your everyday moments. Let His breath fill your lungs.

And when life feels too heavy—wrap up in Him. His promises are sure. His love is without gaps. And sometimes, He'll even paint you a double rainbow just to remind you—He's not done yet.

If you enjoyed this book, will you consider sharing the message with others?

Let us know your thoughts. You can let the author know by visiting or sharing a photo of the cover on our social media pages or leaving a review at a retailer's site. All of it helps us get the message out!

Email: info@ironstreammedia.com

   @ironstreammedia

Iron Stream, Iron Stream Fiction, Iron Stream Kids, and Brookstone Publishing Group, are imprints of Iron Stream Media, which derives its name from Proverbs 27:17, "As iron sharpens iron, so one person sharpens another." This sharpening describes the process of discipleship, one to another. With this in mind, Iron Stream Media provides a variety of solutions for churches, ministry leaders, and nonprofits ranging from in-depth Bible study curriculum and Christian book publishing to custom publishing and consultative services.

For more information on ISM and its imprints, please visit IronStreamMedia.com

www.ingramcontent.com/pod-product-compliance
Lightning Source LLC
Chambersburg PA
CBHW061651120626
46550CB00003B/910